HOLLYWOOD
DAYS,
HOLLYWOOD
NIGHTS

BEN STEIN

HOLLYWOOD DAYS,

HOLLYWOOD NIGHTS

THE DIARY OF A
MAD SCREENWRITER

BANTAM BOOKS
TORONTO · NEW YORK · LONDON · SYDNEY · AUCKLAND

HOLLYWOOD DAYS, HOLLYWOOD NIGHTS

A Bantam Book / July 1988

Grateful acknowledgement is made for permission to reprint the following:
"My Generation," words and music by Peter Townshend.
Copyright © 1965 by Fabulous Music Ltd., London, England.
International Copyright Secured. All rights reserved.
TRO-Devon Music, Inc., New York, controls all publication
rights for the U.S.A. and Canada. Used by permission.
"Ohio" written by Neil Young. Copyright © 1970 by Cotillion Music, Inc.
and Broken Arrow Music. Used by permission. All rights reserved.

LIBRARY OF CONGRESS

Library of Congress Cataloging-in-Publication Data

Stein, Benjamin, 1944—
  Hollywood days, Hollywood nights : the diary of a mad screenwriter
Ben Stein.
    p.   cm.
  ISBN 0-553-34520-6
  1. Stein, Benjamin, 1944— —Diaries.   2. Hollywood (Los Angeles,
Calif.)—Social life and customs.   3. Screenwriters—United States—
Diaries.   4. Authors, American—20th century—Diaries.   I. Title
PS3569.T36Z468   1966
818'.5403—dc19
[B]   88-983
                                                                    CIP

Published simultaneously in the United States and Canada

Bantam Books are published by Bantam Books, a division of Bantam Doubleday Dell Publishing Group,
Inc. Its trademark, consisting of the words "Bantam Books" and the portrayal of a rooster, is Registered
in U.S. Patent and Trademark Office and in other countries. Marca Registrada. Bantam Books, 666
Fifth Avenue, New York, New York 10103.

PRINTED IN THE UNITED STATES OF AMERICA

O   0 9 8 7 6 5 4 3 2 1

For Barron Thomas and for Jim Bellows

This diary is authentic. It is not a novel disguised as a diary. It represents and is my real life, although some names and other unimportant details have been changed. The persons to thank for the diary are the persons to thank for my life—for the parts of it that are interesting and worthwhile, the parts that mimic fantasy.

Above all, I thank my goddess wife, Alexandra, who puts up with a lot from me. There are no better friends in the world than Al and Sally Burton and Sid Dauman. Thank you. The most creative, fun-loving woman in the universe, inventor of the TV movie, DeAnne Barkley, made this book possible by sharing with me her extraordinary view of Hollywood. (I am still a marginal player at best.) I am her debtor.

My assistants and friends come and go, talking not of Michelangelo but of men and clothes and dough. I love them all. Mara Trafficante, Michelle Trafficante, my beloved Valley Girl, Juliette Capretta, her uniquely sweet sister, Daniella Capretta, Vicki Stewart, now Vicki Chickering, Christi Haydon, a Texas beauty who would make a Porsche dealer kick out a Carrera window, Ann-Marie, too kind and lovely to believe, yet somehow real, Susan Reifer, my wistful, lovely, brainoed-out colleague—I love you all.

Michael and Marian Chinich, and their handsome, genius son, Jordan, are fellow travelers in the questioning of daily insanity here, toilers in the celluloid vineyard, cheerful iconoclasts of cinema icons. You're family.

John Hughes made me a famous nerd. It's a lot better than being an obscure nerd, and I thank him. Without his vision, I would not have had the best days of my life. Paul Hirsch kept me in the movie. Thanks, pal.

Steve Green keeps me posted on life among the singles and among the sharp-witted and sharp-tongued. Thanks, buddy.

Eric Alter told me a story that has helped me to understand Hollywood. Thank you.

Rich Procter inspires me with his sense of humor and his sincerity in an insincere world.

In New York, Art Cooper and Eliot Kaplan of *GQ* originally used many of the entries here for a series of my diary entries. Peter Bloch of *Penthouse* commissioned one particularly juicy entry. Lois Wallace persisted in encouraging me to write more. Stephen Rubin of Bantam did the most important part—he published the book.

When I look back on that year, I see most vividly the faces of the sweet kids at Birmingham High School. They restored my faith in life. I despair for the education they are getting, but I love them a lot, and I still cry when I think of their hopeful faces. Goodbye, kids. Remember this little lesson from my parents: there are only two kinds of people: the live and the dead, and living at all is the best revenge. Play on the sand, kiddies, and frisk with your dog, but remember, the bottom of the sea is cruel. Hart Crane said that, and he was right.

NOVEMBER 13, 1985

Ten in the morning. A telephone call from my pal Larry D. just as I was about to feed Martha, Trixie, and Ginger their special veterinarian's mixture of dog food. "Read today's *L.A. Times*," said my pal. "There's an incredible story in it about Joan Didion telling a big crowd of people in New York about how she can remember exactly how rancid the butter smelled on the train to San Francisco. People paid a thousand bucks each to hear her. *A thousand bucks.*"

I read the article. All of the important writers in the whole world were at that gathering of P.E.N. in New York. I was home with Trixie, Martha, and Ginger. Still in my pajamas. Just to show myself that I still retained some minor control over my life, I did something rare. I made absolutely certain that each dog was served her food in the precise dish that had her name on it. I know the dogs can't read. But I can.

Lunch at noon at Universal with my friend H., a studio official responsible for a little item called *Miami Vice*. Two years ago, my friend H. was a wreck, a frustrated novelist writing the same first forty pages of a novel about a black baseball player and a white heiress over and over again. Now he is on the studio payroll at two hundred bills per year, sitting atop the hottest show on TV.

"I'm not gonna lie about this," H. said. "My wife's father's best friend is really a hot agent. He got me in the door. That's the way Hollywood works."

We ate and watched Lew Wasserman eat. It looked to me as if we basically did it the same.

"So I was down in Miami, and Don Johnson wants to direct the next episode of the show, and the producer says, 'Sorry, Don, but we already hired this guy, Fred Finortner or something, to do the next episode. He's really hot in episodic television.' And Don just looks at the producer and says, '*He's* hot?' They got the point. Don's doing the episode."

"So, what's next for you?" I asked my friend.

"I'd like to direct, maybe a few episodes and then a feature," H. said. "I think features are where it's at."

"You have any of that money you owe me?"

"As soon as I do my first feature," H. said, and then I left.

NOVEMBER 14, 1985

Most mornings this month, I drive out the Ventura Freeway to a high school in Van Nuys. It is a huge, sprawling complex that was a veterans' hospital until the United States temporarily ran low on freshly wounded veterans.

I sit in on several classes, including one with genuinely smart, funny kids. My plan is to write a book about high school and why kids come out not knowing anything.

In my favorite class, an attractive woman teacher likes to tell the students about her dreams. "Do you ever dream about, you know, doing it?" one student asks this morning.

"Why, Chris," says the teacher, batting her eyelashes.

"Seriously, the big O," says another student, also male.

"Well, I dream a lot about Don Johnson," the teacher says. "And also about the Lakers."

"Far out," shouts Chris.

"All right, class, that's enough of that," says the teacher. The students then spend the rest of the day discussing the obvious fact that all rich people are Republicans and all poor, working-class people are Democrats. Several of the students want to know if there are exceptions, and if the Republicans are only the rich people, how do they get enough votes to win elections.

"I don't know," says the teacher. "We'll have to look into that someday."

After class, I talk to the teacher. "These are really smart kids. Have you ever thought about giving them something extremely, totally awesomely hard to do, and then seeing if it stretched their minds so they became smarter people?"

The teacher looks at me blankly. "No, I haven't."

"Why not?"

"It's not in my lesson plan," she says, and walks out of the room.

I will have to ask her to show me where the Lakers are in her lesson plan.

NOVEMBER 15, 1985

A meeting with a medium-level studio executive on the West Side. It is almost impossible to get meetings with high studio executives any longer, at least for me. Every single studio is in a state of confusion. On every lot there are firings, retrenchings, leveraged buy-outs, rumors of acquisitions, and the dread news of steadily dropping ticket sales.

I sat in a windowless office and spun out my proposed story. "There's this lady D.A. and a good-looking tough Irish street cop in Boston, see, and they're in love. The only problem is that the cop's married to this righteous bitch who's a total shit. She won't divorce him, and she says that if he tries to divorce her, she'll tell the cardinal and the police commissioner and the mayor, and his career'll be ruined. So the cop and the D.A. murder the wife, and then the best friend catches them and has to turn them in."

"I don't know," the studio official says. "Where's the jeopardy?"

"The jeopardy for the wife is that she gets killed. The jeopardy for the cop is that he'll get caught. Ditto for the lady D.A. For the best friend, it hurts to turn in his best pal."

"Yeah, but where's the motive for the murder?"

"The bitch won't give him a divorce."

"That's not enough motive."

"The bitch is going to ruin his career, ruin his girlfriend's career, and keep him apart from the woman he loves for the rest of his life."

"That's still not enough motive," said the studio executive, alternately flexing his muscles and paring his nails with a penknife.

"Well, what would be enough motive?"

"There's only one motive that anyone at this studio will believe," he said. "Money."

"Okay, so the wife has some money, and that's why the husband kills her."

"Fine," the studio executive said. "Now we have a story."

On the way home, I stopped at the Chalet Gourmet. Steak is fifteen dollars per pound. Fresh salmon is fifteen dollars per pound. I have no idea how I can afford any of these items. I have no idea how I can afford anything.

At the bakery counter, I saw my longtime pal Dolly. Let's be honest about this: Dolly is a hooker. She started out with a view to making enough money to buy a seat on the New York Stock Exchange. Now she wants to have a nail salon. That's what Los Angeles does to you.

With Dolly was a petite, adorable blond girl named Laraine. She had hair down to her waist.

"This is my new associate," Dolly said. "Isn't she cute?"

"Gorgeous," I said. "What do you do in your spare time?" I asked while we looked at the cupcakes.

"I work as a paralegal," she said. "It's really great work, but I need some extra money. I want to buy my own airplane. A Piper Cherokee."

"And I'm going to help her pay for it," Dolly said. "If you know anyone who'd like to meet Laraine and me, let me know."

"I want that airplane," Laraine said with a wink.

On the way home, after rush hour, the streets were deserted.

I drove along Fairfax and then up to Hollywood Boulevard, past the apartments and the closed, drug addicts' windows. The wind whipped through the royal palms above the sodium vapor street lamps. There were almost no other cars except an occasional Toyota Cressida driven by an Asian woman who stared straight ahead.

On the radio, through my magnificent stereo, a shriek. "People try to put us down. Just because we get around. Things they do look awful cold. Hope I die before I get old."

You can count on it, boys.

I turned up Outpost, past the old Spanish-style mansions abutting the ancient street lamps and the empty street. I had the fantasy I often have when the streets are deserted in Los Angeles: the United States has just lost a world war. The next morning, the first Soviet occupation troops will arrive. This is the end, the last moment of Los Angeles civilization. The Mercedes, the palm trees, the rock 'n' roll, the call girls working for a million-dollar airplane, the fresh salmon flown in from Norway for us, the gorgeous dome of day for night that is Los Angeles is enshrined in a crystal paperweight, about to be smashed on the floor, to dribble out into eternity, and vanish.

What's the answer? Turn up the stereo. "I'm not tryin' to cause a big seh-seh-seh-sensation. Just talkin' 'bout my geh-geh-generation."

NOVEMBER 16, 1985

I wasn't going to tell you about this, but I think you should know. Every so often I do something unusual. With an organization called Animal Alliance, I take poor abused dogs to branches of a chain of convalescent homes for the elderly in West L.A. The homes are usually small, one-story affairs, mostly because not too many of the guests like to run up and down stairs. They have linoleum floors, and large recreation rooms where the guests sit in wheelchairs and stare listlessly at TV. The homes have an "activities room," which has a few magazines and tattered posters of Aix-en-Provence, and maybe one game of checkers and one of canasta.

The guests are in pajamas with bathrobes. They are really old, far past Ronald Reagan old. They are almost always sick as well, but not critically. Their faces have the look of thin, fragile lampshades in which the bulb is flickering. Their eyes have a dense opacity that looks inward rather than outward. They are old in a way you rarely see on the street or at the Burbank Studios or at Morton's.

They are feeble, weak, unconnected with the freeways usually a few yards from their beds. They are in a linoleum and vinyl waiting room preparing to travel to eternity. You cannot imagine what their hands look like with their veins and purple spots and twitching. They are not the hands of a cute old woman looking for the beef. They are the hands of men and women who know their next step is death.

Martha Wyss, the founder of Animal Alliance, hit on the idea. Her organization collects lost, abandoned, pitiful dogs from all around West L.A. Often they are Dachshunds thrown out onto the freeway, mutts tossed into a trash can wrapped inside a plastic bag, Labs whose master has died, leaving them alone in the world. Animal Alliance takes them in, cares for them, and tries to find masters and mistresses for them. The dogs are lonely and need the human touch while they await adoption, which can be a long wait. Martha thought she might connect the lonely humans with the lonely dogs, and bring the dogs to convalescent homes for the two species to find love.

I wish you could see the looks on the patients' faces when we hold a straight-haired terrier up to their wheelchairs. A flood of animation washes over them. Their torpor vanishes. Their eyes snap into focus. They reach out their hands for the fur. Their hands stop shaking. Suddenly, the old woman who was in a trance is alive, alert, connected with the warm affection of the moment. The man who was lying in bed, on his side, moaning softly, sits up, takes the Dachshund on his lap, and starts to laugh. The whole convalescent home snaps into a kind of excited electricity as the patients follow the dogs in their wheelchairs, find scraps of cookies and cake to give the dogs, start to tell Martha Wyss stories about their own dogs. "When I came home from the Pacific, there he was, waiting in the front room in Tulsa, just as if I had never left." "When my daughter was born, I got her an Irish Setter so she wouldn't be afraid of dogs, and you know that dog stayed by her side when she had measles and wouldn't even let us near her she was so protective. . . ." "I had to give up my Archie when I moved in here. . . ."

So we go slowly from room to room, and the dogs change each room from crypt to living room. The dogs don't get paid, and they don't even have agents. After a few hours, we take the dogs outside and go home. The convalescent homes are invariably silent when we arrive, and we can invariably hear men and women talking and even laughing as we leave.

I take no credit for this. It's all in the love of Martha Wyss, and most of all, in the miracle that is a dog.

NOVEMBER 17, 1985

Long ago and far away, when I was in law school, I had a friend named Carl K. Carl and his wife Joan used to play bridge with me and my wife every night in the third year of law school. We would get outrageously drunk, smoke hundreds of cigarettes, and cheat at cards. Outside, we could see the snow swirling under the street lamps, coating the Oak Street Connector. On our way home we would pass by the New Haven Green and look at the three churches of New England, white clapboard in the snowy winter moonlight. Often, just as Carl and I had made a dishonest small

7

slam, doubled up with laughter, we heard the midnight bells of those churches. We thought we would live forever.

Carl and his wife got divorced right after graduation. Carl lives in Portland now and teaches law. His new wife and he took a chance and had a baby eighteen months ago. The baby had severe, irreparable brain damage. Sometimes the baby would go into one hundred seizures per hour. I called Carl every week, and then one day Carl told me it was too sad to talk about any longer, so I stopped calling.

This morning I had to call a mutual friend in San Francisco. "What's with Carl?" I asked. "Any change with his daughter?"

"I guess I didn't tell you," my mutual friend said. "Carl's daughter died about six months ago. Maybe longer. Now his wife's pregnant again. She's forty-two, but they're just gonna get right back up on the horse and try again."

"Very brave," I said.

"Yes, listen, I have another call and then my wife and I are going to look at sailboats. Can I call you back?"

My wife was at the manicurist. I sat out by the pool all morning and closed my eyes. I tried to hear the sound of those bells from the New Haven Green at midnight in the snow on a night when we all knew we were going to live forever. But all I could hear was the sound of the fake machine-gun fire from the "Mr. T" exhibit on the Universal Tour at the bottom of the hill, then the dogs barking in alarm. When I opened my eyes, all I could see was the smog over the Valley, and that the pool man hadn't really done a good job cleaning out the Jacuzzi. It was still filled with pine needles from the Santa Anas of the night before. On the trip between living forever and being dead forever, that is what you collect if you live in Los Angeles: a Jacuzzi filled with pine needles.

NOVEMBER 18, 1985

Enough brooding! Something good has finally happened!

This afternoon I went with my partner, Schmuel, to pitch my favorite story at a studio. The story is about the three civil rights workers who were slaughtered by the Ku Klux Klan in Philadelphia, Mississippi, in June 1964. Goodman, Chaney, and Schwerner. Last year I met an airplane salesman who had been a Mississippi state trooper and knew facts about the case no one else knew. I optioned his rights, and have been trying for about one year to sell this damned thing. The additional selling point I have picked up is that James Chaney, the black twenty-one-year-old illiterate painter's helper who gave his life so people could either vote or not vote as they chose, was a mimic. He could do a white sheriff, a black mammy, even a Harvard civil rights volunteer. A natural comedian. Skull battered so badly by the Klan that he was unrecognizable even by his family. I think there's a movie in that somewhere.

Anyway, I have now pitched this everywhere. Everywhere I have gotten a respectful hearing, but the usual verdict is that it's too heavy for today's disintegrating market.

Today, I pitched to a man wearing a silk pajama top and wool slacks, working standing up at a rolltop desk like a Studio City version of Joseph Welch.

"I cannot believe what a great story that is," the executive said. "It's just fantastic. Really great."

"I'm so glad you like it," I said.

"It's the ultimate youth picture. About kids who do something and make a difference."

"So true."

"Do you think we'll have legal problems? I mean with the Ku Klux Klan?"

9

"I think we can solve them," I said gently.

"Fuck 'em anyway. We'll do it anyway. It's just too good to miss. That's how good it is."

You see, there is hope for eternal life after all.

NOVEMBER 19, 1985

A telephone call from T., the "executive assistant" to the man in the silk pajamas.

"Can we just put that Mississippi thing on hold for a few days?" he asked.

"What's the problem?"

"The problem is that my boss thinks maybe it's too heavy for today's youth market. Can you just give us a few days to think about it?"

"Take your time."

"You understand we still love the story and we still love you, don't you?"

"Of course."

"Say hello to the kids."

I don't have any kids.

NOVEMBER 20, 1985

What is so rare as a perfect day?

About three months ago, maybe more, I went to visit my friend Michael Chinich. Michael is a handsome rogue who serves mankind as president of the John Hughes Company. In that capacity, he works as producer on the John Hughes current movie in production, *Ferris Bueller's Day Off*. Who knows if it will be as big as John Hughes's other movies: *Mr. Mom, The Breakfast Club,* and *National Lampoon's Vacation?*

John Hughes, a tall braino with wire-rimmed glasses and that air of sure winner that Hollywood people on a roll, mergers and acquisitions tycoons, and twenty-game winners have, heard me talking to Michael Chinich.

To make a long story short, Hughes asked me if I cared to do a voice-over of a teacher during a scene in a high school classroom. When I got to the set and started reading my lines, the student extras began to laugh. John Hughes began to laugh. Even Tak Fujimoto, the cinematographer, began to laugh.

"It's great," John Hughes said. "Your voice is so boring. It's like every teacher we've ever had and hated. It's fantastic. How would you like to be on camera?"

"I'd love to," I said truthfully.

The scene was reshot to give me about twice as many lines, this time on camera.

Again, the students and the crew began to laugh like madmen. John Hughes huddled with his producers, nodded several times, then came over to me.

"How would you like to do a whole ten-minute monologue on camera?" he asked. "Just you talking about something, anything, for ten minutes, but make it really, really boring, and pretend you're talking to a whole roomful of really bored kids."

"I shall do my best," I said.

For ten unbroken minutes, with the camera rolling, I talked about how the Smoot-Hawley tariff bill came about, how supply-siders believe that Smoot-Hawley caused the Great Depression, and about how most mainstream economists think that is nonsense. Bear in mind that in my parents' house, that kind of conversation is considered not only not comically boring, but extremely exciting and even controversial.

But on Sound Stage 16 at Paramount Pictures, the cast and crew were in a shock of hilarity. They giggled. They covered their mouths. They slapped each other on the back silently as the Panaflex pointed my way.

When I got to the Laffer Curve, the laughing on the set became so loud that the director had to stop shooting. He shouted "cut," waved to the cast and crew, and they began to applaud. Not just a smattering, but real applause. Matthew Broderick, the star of the show, walked up to me, shook my hand, and said, "That was wonderful. What else have you been in?"

I have no idea whether my scene will stay in the movie. I have no realistic hope that the afternoon on Stage 16 will change my life. This is what I do know: on most days I wonder what I'm doing in Los Angeles, why classmates from college who cannot add and subtract are making ten million dollars a year in junk bonds, why I have never even been invited to be a *member* of P.E.N., let alone speak about the rancidity of butter in front of thousand-dollar-a-pop listeners, how I am going to pay for the pool man, and why I have wasted my one and only life. Today was different.

November 21, 1985

Fact: Everyone in Los Angeles is sick all the time. About five years ago, a virus arrived from Thailand or Zihuantanejo or Ogaden. Everyone in town got infected. The symptoms are headache, fatigue, sore throat, nausea, dizziness, and irritability. The L.A. flu is as hard to get rid of as greed. Once you have it, you have it forever.

As usual this morning, I was awakened by Trixie, Martha, and Ginger stretching and scratching under the covers of the bed. I took them out and felt light-headed. My wife staggered out of the bedroom. "I have a sore throat," she said.

Luisa, the daughter of our housekeeper, Elena, called to say that Elena did not feel well and would not be in.

Sara, my Valley Girl friend and sometime assistant, called to say that she had nausea and would not come in. Sara looks a lot like the young Audrey Hepburn with makeup and Esprit clothes. "The hell with that," I said. "Get in here right away."

"Okay," she said cheerfully. "In fact, I feel a lot better already."

That's one of the things about the L.A. flu. It comes and goes depending on what you have to do that day or whether you are just going to be spending another day wishing you were Michael Eisner.

Sara arrived just as I was writing the end of a letter to the Securities and Exchange Commission. Did I tell you that I am engaged in endless litigation with a company in which I own enough shares to pay for one good meal at La Scala? It's so complicated that it's enough to make you light-headed, but eventually I'm going to win and give back to those suckers some of the aggravation they and all their pig kind have dished out to me.

Anyway, Sara arrived. She hurled herself through the door to my office as if the entire Wehrmacht were in hot pursuit, flung herself on my couch, almost smothering Martha, and then looked up.

"God I love this dog," she said.

"Me, too."

NOVEMBER 23, 1985

I forgot to tell you something. On my perfect day on Sound Stage 16 when I played a teacher, in my make-believe class were three gorgeous extras. After my monologue, I sat down with two of them, Cassie and Marcie. Cassie was your usual ravishingly beautiful blond California girl with blue eyes, full red lips, and a cagey look in her blue eyes. Marcie was different. She was a street-waif, tough-girl, white-under-the-pupil blue eyes look of unmixed cunning. She was fourteen. She couldn't get over what a great job I had done on my part. All she ever wanted in life was to act. She hoped I would remember her. She rubbed my ankle with her ankle and giggled. She was fourteen.

Tonight, Saturday, John Hughes held the wrap party for *Ferris Bueller's Day Off*. We all drank and ate in the upstairs lounge of The Palace. It's a Hollywood nightclub for the twenty- to twenty-five-year-old set. We adults watched them from a balcony, talked gross participation, and tried to seem important.

"Sunrise," a powerful woman executive at the studio, swept in wearing a full-length leather trenchcoat of impenetrable black. She shook my hand but kept her elbow rigid to make sure that she did not actually have to kiss me. Frank Mancuso, the chairman of the board, came in, hugged John Hughes, beamed at everyone else, then left. Ned Tanen appeared. He's the head of production. He looked around, ate one raw shrimp, complimented Sunrise on her coat, and then left.

I sat talking to Michael Chinich about what hotels have the best bathrooms. Suddenly Marcie appeared at my side, steaming with rage, cunning blue eyes ringed with Goebbels white and tinged with red. She began to swing her denimed leg against my leg under the tablecloth. "I am so mad," she said. "I was downstairs with Cassie, and these two older men started dancing with us. Two of them. I mean they're so much older."

"How old?"

"Twenty-one, twenty-two," she sulked. "I'm only fourteen. Fourteen. I mean, these guys look at me, and I know what they want. But they're looking at a fourteen-year-old, and even though I may look older, I'm just fourteen, and they may all want to, you know, get me in trouble, but they aren't allowed to."

"What kind of trouble?"

"You know. They just want me for a one-night stand. I could get into a lot of trouble. I've had friends who got pregnant, who really got messed up by guys who didn't care at all about them, who just wanted to use their bodies. But look at me," she said, holding forward her little body, wrapped tightly in jeans and a red T-shirt. "I may look like somebody to be used, but I don't want to be used."

"Why not?"

"Because I want a man to know me, to value me for who I am. Is that so wrong? I don't want a man to just take advantage of me no matter how available, how ready I might look. After all, I'm only fourteen." She giggled and made her lips into a pout. "That means, don't touch. Not even if you really want to. Not unless you're willing to get to know me."

There was a long pause.

"So tell me, Marcie," I said. "What law school do you think you'd like to go to?"

NOVEMBER 24, 1985

My old pal John Gregory Dunne once said that Los Angeles has the worst climate in the world. Unfortunately, he was not completely wrong. The climate here in winter is often wet, foggy, cold, and featureless except for more of the same. Last night a freezing rain fell all through the night. There was actually a thin sheen of ice on the flagstone next to the swimming pool.

Today is Sunday, the most miserable day of the week. On most days you can feel the energy of ambition and self-obsession ripping out of the one-room apartments, the acting schools, the telephone boiler rooms, the used-car lots, the wholesale jewelry showrooms, the artists' lofts, and zigzagging across the sky like lightning. On Sundays, especially rainy, foggy Sundays, the city is sleeping it off. The whole binge of delusion, aggression, and sales that is a week of L.A. life turns into a dull headache of remorse and fear that keeps people in bed, or in front of the Sony watching the Raiders, fitfully lapsing into a trance of confused bewilderment before the next onslaught.

I got out of bed, got dressed, and drove down to the Paramount lot. Now that I am John Hughes's new best friend, I have carte blanche to go onto his stages. Today, the prom scene from yet another John Hughes movie, *Pretty in Pink*, was being shot on Sound Stage 13. I arrived just as the morning's shooting ended. The cast of eighty teenage extras in tuxedoes and prom gowns marched through the rain to Stage 15 to have their lunch.

To really love Hollywood, you have to see what I saw at lunch: Outside the studio gates, the world is wrapped in cold, wet, gray fog. It is a nothing day, a day hardly worth being alive for. Inside the studio, in a freezing-cold open sound stage, eighty kids are happily chirping, eating crab legs, filet mignon, creole blackfish, baked potatoes, string beans, chocolate pudding, chocolate fudge sundaes, fresh apple pie, fresh apples, sugar cookies, and carrot cake. The cast and crew are all talking about the lights, the sets, other shoots, what they will do when this picture is finished, what they will do when they start their next picture, how they will continue to revolve in the gilded world within a world that is Hollywood movie-making.

I sat down across from Jean Webber. She is an artist from Minneapolis who painted for several years in a loft in Williamsburg, Brooklyn, then became a production designer in Hollywood.

"This is a totally separate world," Jean said. "It works inside a nucleus of a cell. The people who work here aren't working in everyone else's reality. They're re-creating their own reality, which will exist only for them for about eight months until the rest of the world gets to play in it, too. So they're removed from the world not only by space but also by time."

Jean has big blue eyes and silky blond hair. She is too smart to look that good.

"Also, people here basically only relate to each other. They have a whole set of words and connections and skills that aren't really valued anywhere else in the world, but they're extraordinarily valuable here," I said.

Steve, Jean's boyfriend and the first assistant director, added, "Plus, everybody here has an idea of what pay should be that's completely unique to the picture business. It just doesn't figure in any other business."

Steve and Jean left to set up the scene for after lunch. I felt a rustling next to me. It was Marcie. In a black, extremely low-cut prom dress. She was swinging her leg back and forth, rubbing against me. Maybe I'm taking that too personally. Maybe it's just her way of "tuning her instrument" before the next shot.

"We stayed up until three A.M. last night," Marcie said. "Talking about these boys we met at The Palace and what they wanted to do with me."

"Are you in every picture John Hughes makes?" I asked.

"My mom has a friend at the casting company," Marcie said. "That's all. I've never met John Hughes. You should have seen those boys. Well, not really boys. More like men. You can't imagine all the things they wanted to do with me."

"But you're only fourteen, right?"

"Right. And they might look at me and see something they like," she said, pouting and batting her fourteen-year-old eyelashes, "but I'm too young. I'm really just a little girl."

"Just out of a silly curiosity," I said, "how did you know what things those men wanted to do with you? Did they tell you?"

Marcie looked at me as if she were Einstein answering a question about tenth-grade algebra. "Oh, I think I know what men think about when they look at me. Don't you think I know it? I mean, there's really only one thing they could be thinking about. But they can't do it. Not yet. Not unless they really know me. I'm only fourteen."

"I see. Let me ask you this. Have you got enough municipal bonds in your portfolio?"

NOVEMBER 25, 1985

This is my birthday. Forty-one. I don't like it. I would much rather be younger. When I was thirty-one and felt as if my life were completely stuck, I felt as if I could always try again. There was time enough. *Hay tiempo*, as the valet parkers tell me when I'm looking for my car. Now, I see the sands running out as if each fucking grain of sand were going to collect a two-million-dollar lottery ticket at the bottom of the hourglass. Scary.

I went out to eat with a lawyer. We talked about leveraged buy-outs. I'm against them for a lot of good legal reasons. I'm also against them for a good human reason: I'm sick of seeing everyone else somehow contrive to loot the system, while I'm trying to figure out if I can pay my MasterCard. The lawyer told me about his work saving the first mortgage bondholders of the New Haven Railroad back in 1976. He told me I should become a lawyer again. God help me, I ate my salmon teriyaki lunch and I actually thought about it. A lot.

Then I drove over the San Diego Freeway to Century City to see my shrink. A famous one. An M.D. with superfamous, superrich patients. Corporate machers, studio heads. The kind of people who know how to loot the system. He plays the saxophone between patients, collects Knoll figurines, and at one time was considering working as a physician in Afghanistan. He's one helluva sensitive guy, like me.

About fifteen minutes into the session, he offered a little piece of gossip. The shrink happened to have heard at an exclusive dinner party in Bel-Air last week that *Krypto*, a movie whose outline I had written, which is scheduled for production in January, had been dropped from the schedule. "They're afraid it'll be considered too anti-Soviet," he said. "They're worried about that. That's what I heard." He looked sad.

I could only gasp for about two minutes. *Krypto* is the first and only movie I have ever been connected with that was definitely set for production. I have been here nine years, and this was my one big shot. Plus, I need the money. I have not earned any real money in a good long time. I still spend it as if I were earning it by the ton. I just don't earn it any longer. Let's keep it a secret from Morton's, Spago, Merlin Olsen Porsche, and Bullock's Wilshire.

"You're kidding," I croaked to my shrink.

He fingered his saxophone, which he always keeps by his regulation brown leather chair, and looked even sadder. "I wish I were," he sighed.

I staggered across his office to his telephone and began to call:
The head of the studio. Out to lunch.
The head of legal. In New York.
The head of business affairs. He'll call back.
The agent who made the deal. Out for the day.
The agent who heads TV. Out playing tennis.
The TV writer for the *Herald-Examiner*.
The TV writer for the *L.A. Times*.
The head of TV movies at NBC.
The head of TV movies at ABC.
The head of CAA.
The head of ICM.
The head of Leading Artists.
All in meetings.

I had in my mind an image of the water in a bathtub one second after the plug is pulled. It hesitates for an instant, not quite sure that nothing is holding it up any longer. Then it starts to swirl around in a circle and then it vanishes down the drain, and pretty soon there is nothing there any longer. That's me, I thought. That's my whole life.

I looked over at my shrink, guiltily fingering his saxophone. *You did this on purpose because you're jealous.*

Another call to the head of business affairs. "I'll hold."

Steve came on the line. "Well," I asked in a rush. "Is it true? Are you dropping *Krypto*?"

"No way," he said. "We love that movie. No way."

"Really?" I demanded. "Really?"

"I'm head of business affairs, and I haven't heard about it," he said smoothly.

"Okay, well, just checking," I said.

The shrink carefully adjusted his cuffs. "This is very interesting. You see, the man who told me that *Krypto* was dead has just had his deal at the same studio dropped. So perhaps that made him simply feel negatively about everything at the studio. He has a habit of exaggerating things. Also of distorting facts to make himself look more important and other people look small."

Oh you creep.

"I think you might have told me that before you told me the project was dead. It was the single worst piece of news I've ever gotten, Doctor."

"You're right," he said. "I might well have made a mistake. We have an unusual relationship, and I don't know exactly how to handle it."

"I'll say."

"Look, if you learn anything more about this, will you call me?"

"No, Doctor, I don't think I will."

"I don't blame you."

"I should think not."

"By the way, happy birthday."

November 26, 1985

This afternoon I drove out to Birmingham High School in my shining, gleaming Porsche. The sun came screaming down onto the Ventura Freeway and then bounced off *mein weinrote metallike* Porsche finish. I pulled past the chain link fence that surrounds the school, nodded at the black guard who maintains the school as a closed campus, and pulled into my space right in front of the principal's office. Class was changing, and the students looked hungrily at my car.

Pretty good. Pretty goddamn good. Here I am in high school with a wine-red metallic Porsche 928 on this glorious day. Can't beat it with a stick. A boy with a blue leather jacket and his girlfriend with orange hair and orange tights called out to me, "Hey, buddy, buff car."

So you see. I'm forty-one and I'm in high school with my great car, and what could be wrong?

Today I was scheduled to lecture an advanced placement English class on "Writing as a Profession." The boys and girls in the class are *really smart*. They read *Vanity Fair*. The novel by Thackeray, not the magazine by Tina Brown. They know about existentialism. They know the difference between a roman à clef and a novel of manners. They know what *picaresque* means. They are all neatly dressed in Benetton colors. Each one is in for early decision at Yale or Stanford or Dartmouth or Georgetown.

"I write a lot of different forms," I said cheerfully. "Novels, financial books, magazine articles, occasional scripts. Lots of things. Sometimes outlines for TV shows. I try to keep myself active in a variety of forms so that I can sort of cross-pollinate myself, heh-heh."

The students looked up at me with their earnest faces and

21

then the teacher invited questions. A thicket of hands shot up. I called on one frail-looking young woman with red-rimmed glasses and a trembling lower lip.

"In your kind of writing," she asked, "which pays the most?"

"Well, writing for the movies pays the most, but it offers very little in the way of creative satisfaction," I said.

"Well, exactly how much does it pay?" a male student with a letter jacket wanted to know. "As much as being a lawyer?"

"It all depends on the lawyer and the writer."

The students looked thoughtful for a moment and then another boy had a question: "Can you help me get a meeting at a studio? I have a really great idea for a movie set in a high school."

"Does anyone have a question about writing that doesn't have to do with money?" the teacher asked.

The students looked puzzled for a moment and then one girl looked up brightly. "Can you explain to me what deferred compensation is? My dad is always complaining about that. What is it anyway? Does it have anything to do with money?"

"Let me ask a question," I countered. "Is there anyone in this room who would want to be a writer if there wasn't any money in it? Who might just want to write to express yourself, say, in a magazine article?"

Again, there was a moment's pause and then a student raised her hand. It was the same one who had the trembling lower lip and the red, braino glasses. "What magazines pay the most?" she asked, holding her pencil poised above her white three-holed paper with its aquamarine lines. "Could you run down the top five or ten?"

Dinner at Morton's with Lucinda DeMott. Lucy is a woman in her early fifties. She is credited with inventing the entire idea of the nighttime soap opera while she was at ABC many years ago. Now she is an executive at a production company. She comes from a famous Charleston, South Carolina, family. She has been married five times and has eight children. She is the source of some of the most extraordinary quotes I have ever heard. My favorite was when I gave her a gift of a VCR in return for a large favor she had done for me. (Well, getting me a rewrite on a mini, to tell the truth.)

"Thank you," she said with a perfectly straight face. "Now I can be happy."

Maybe that's not my favorite quote from her. Maybe my favorite quote was when she told me about a young cowboy who treated her badly but whom she loved anyway. "I don't care how people feel about me. I only care how I feel about them."

Or maybe it was the time when one of her sons was injured after a surfing accident off Point Dume. "As long as I can feel sorry for him and not feel sorry for myself, I'll be all right," she said.

Lucy is a genius.

Lucy took my wife and me out to dinner for my birthday. Not only that, but she had a gift. Neatly wrapped in green Christmas wrapping paper with a red bow were forty-one California Lottery tickets. "If we scratch our way through dinner," she said, "we can wind up rich."

We started to scratch. My wife's secretary had won five thousand dollars one week before. I figured it was my turn.

"I just want to know something," I said. "When I came out here, I was a pretty hot item. Deals all over the place. New kid in town. Now I can't get arrested. What's going on?"

"It's because of luck," she said. "You either have it or you don't. That's the trick."

We ordered our dinners and scratched. Alex won two dollars. Lucy won two dollars. I won nothing.

NOVEMBER 27, 1985

In the fall of 1981 I flew up to San Jose en route to my dream town, Santa Cruz on the Monterey Bay. Next to me on PSA Flight 87 was a beautiful girl with green eyes, curly brown hair, and a sweet, childish pout. She also had a chest that would make Hugh Hefner have a second stroke. She looked over at me curiously while I read the stock market page of *The Wall Street Journal* to measure my goddamn losses.

"What's all that little type?" she asked. "And all those little numbers?"

"Those are stock market quotes."

"What's a stock market quote?" she asked.

"That's where you get told the prices of stocks that get traded on Wall Street."

"What's Wall Street?"

"It's a street in New York where all the corporate finance people hang out."

"What does that mean? What do they do when they hang out? Do they get blown out on coke, or what?"

Stacey was the child's name. She was seventeen. She was going up to see her boyfriend in Lake Tahoe and ski. We talked the whole way up. We became pals. When she got back to L.A., I took her to lunch at Mr. Chow. I took her to read for a part with my pal Michael. She flunked. She was a senior in a Valley high school. She was adorable.

One day she came over when I was talking to my parents in Washington, D.C. When I got off the phone, I told her whom I had been talking to and where they lived.

"Oh, in Washington. Where it rains all the time," she exclaimed.

"No, in Washington, D.C. You're thinking of Washington State."

"What's the difference?" Stacey asked cheerfully.

"One is the capital of the United States," I said. "The other is a state in the Pacific Northwest."

"Really?" Stacey said. "Which is which?"

Another time, when I was watching *Guadalcanal Diary* on TV, Stacey asked me who the little soldiers with slanty eyes were.

"Well, let's try to figure it out," I said in my best schoolteacher manner. "What countries did we fight against in World War II?"

"Germany?"

"Yes, but who else?"

"Russia?"

"No, Stacey. Russia was on our side. Who did we fight against in the Pacific?"

Stacey wrinkled up her adorable nose and scrunched her eyes to show she was thinking hard.

"Germany?"

"No, Stacey. In the Pacific. Who did we fight against in the Pacific?"

"Russia?"

"No, we fought against Japan. That's who those little guys with the slanty eyes are. Japanese."

"You're kidding," Stacey gasped. "We fought against Japan? Who won?"

Like most California children, she went to schools that baby-sat but did not teach, watched TV instead of reading books, and planned only on the future being better than the past.

Only a few months after I met Stacey, I placed an ad in the placement office at a junior college in the Valley, for a go-fer, messengerette assistant. The first girl who appeared at the house was Traci. She was and is a tall, olive-skinned, young beauty. She has a domineering, overpowering attitude that masks the heart of a child. She's been with me since that day as employee and now as friend. She is not the same as Sara, but similar.

Once I started to tell Traci about how Stacey didn't know the difference between Washington, D.C., and Washington State. "That's a hard question," Traci said seriously. "Which is which?"

For the last four years, Stacey and Traci have been my closest friends in the whole world. They have told me stories, kept me company while Alex travels or has the flu, called me at 1:00 A.M. with tears about their parents and confessions about boys. I have gotten at least five development deals from them, and a reputation as a man who is hip to what kids want to see and know, which is worth having in the picture business. (The best story was about two call girls who decided to go to USC to find rich husbands and wound up becoming lawyers.)

In return, I helped them with their letters of application to USC, with their term papers on neutralism versus neutrality, with car crashes they couldn't tell their parents about, with getting stranded in Fez, Morocco, without a cent. (They had taken a train there from Madrid at midnight without any money on a dare from a friend in the "USC Abroad" program. I sent them a thousand dollars, which I deducted from their advance on the movie I was sure I would sell about their adventures with the Guardians of Islam in Marrakech, but which I never sold, of course.)

Now they have both graduated from USC. Traci still works for me very rarely as a messengerette and enforcer. Stacey works in Washington, D.C., for a congresswoman. They both miss life at the Gamma Nu house at USC. On Capitol Hill, there is no "rooftesting." That was when the girls of the Gamma Nu would take stereos, televisions, bicycles, mirrors, refrigerators, and clock radios up to the roof of the house and throw them off four stories onto Twenty-Eighth Street below, just to see if they still worked.

So, I am their best friend, their father surrogate, their pal. It is the day before Thanksgiving, and Stacey came to see me at Spago even before she had dinner with her parents. Traci even got there first and told Bernard, the captain, that she was my daughter. She always tells captains and headwaiters that she is my daughter. They are two sweet, touching little girls, and I love them even when they are bad.

We got a good table, right next to the window, and I felt pretty good about being there with my little puppies on the day before Thanksgiving, waiting to learn all about Stacey's life in Washington, D.C., where it only rains some of the time.

Rutger Hauer sat right next to us. Sly Stallone and his new b.f. Brigitte Nielsen sat three tables away, and Stacey had a question, as she ate pizza.

"I keep meeting these guys in Washington who tell me how the Jews run everything and Israel has the U.S. under her thumb. Also, they tell me that nobody can make a move without clearing it with the Jews. And also that the United States gives all this aid to Israel while the Palestinians are starving and everyone blames the PLO for all these murders and stuff when really Israel is doing it just to make trouble. So, Benj, what's the truth?"

For a long moment I felt as if time had stood still and a vile semblance of reality had stolen the love and trust I had felt for Stacey all the years I had known her. I was speechless and crushed, so Stacey went on.

"Like, a guy who works for Representative Bentley from Maryland gave me this book about how the Jews run everything and I started to read it, and it's really scary."

"Stacey, where did you get this horrible stuff? Where do people tell you these disgusting things? What kind of friends do you have?"

I felt a kind of dizziness that you get when you realize that you have just invested four years in building a mousetrap that has just sprung shut on your own neck.

Across the room, Rutger Hauer was slapping Sly Stallone on the back. The two men laughed hilariously while Brigitte Nielsen talked to Wolfgang Puck. It was a festive night.

"I really can't believe the kinds of friends you hang around with," I said. "I'm really angry about this." (Still talking like a father, as you can see.)

"Benj," Stacey said, looking slightly apprehensive as she drank her white wine, "I hate to tell you this, but I hear this from everyone in Washington who's not Jewish. I hear it from aides up on the Hill, and from guys I meet at parties, and guys I meet at bars. They really have it in for Israel."

"Do you understand that it's pure evil, as if they were telling you to drink blood?" I really did not know what to say, and that sounded right.

"I'm trying to keep an open mind," Stacey said. "I want to learn both sides."

"Stacey, darling, do you understand that there is no advantage to keeping an open mind as between good and evil, or between truth and a lie?"

Stacey looked at me candidly and answered. "No. Explain that to me."

(I told you I had to get her through USC.)

Traci looked up from her goat cheese pizza. "Benj, if you think that's bad, you should have seen what was going on at USC. At our sorority the girls totally had it in for Jews. There were three Jewish girls in the sorority compared with a hundred and fifty who weren't Jewish, and even so, the girls were squawking all the time that there were too many Jews. My roommate routinely used to call Lisa Rubin 'Jewgirl' whenever she turned her back. You can't even imagine the kind of stuff they say at the fraternities about the Jewish fraternities."

"This is horrible," I said. "Just terrible."

"Yeah, but this is the way it is," Traci said. "It's because all the Jews are so rich and so pushy."

"What are you talking about? I'm Jewish. You got through school because of me. How can you possibly talk like that? How do you think that makes me feel after all the things my wife and I have done for you?"

"Yeah," Traci said, "but you're not really Jewish. You're not like most Jewish people at all, and Alex isn't Jewish at all. She probably wouldn't be surprised at what we're saying."

"First of all, I'm every bit as Jewish as the guys with the fur hats and the yarmulkes on La Brea Boulevard. Every bit. Don't try that crap on me. Second, if Alex heard you talking this way, she'd probably kill you right on the spot."

Stacey and Traci looked chastised, almost guilty as they slurped at their drinks. Then, as if joined by a telepathic link, they both spoke up. "It's not that we really believe any of that stuff," Traci said. "That's just what we heard. We just want you to know what's going on out there."

"Yeah, we don't agree with those people," Traci said with a concerned smile. "We just wanted to help you learn about how the world works."

Thank you, girls. You have.

NOVEMBER 28, 1985

Thanksgiving. Our friends Carl and Cora had a dinner. Turkey. A special dressing made with garlic. Five different desserts made without sugar. A game of Trivial Pursuit. A new Audi 5000S Turbo in the driveway. The parents sneaking out to the garage to smoke cigarettes while the son, Aaron, a redheaded twelve-year-old, studies the stock market page of the *L.A. Times*. The perfect evening for the post-Woodstock generation.

By the way, I hate and loathe Trivial Pursuit. It is the perfect game for the age of stupidity. The concept that knowing the name of Lionel Richie's biggest song has any particular value is an assault on the idea of knowledge itself. Plus, whoever made up the categories for one stupid version of this stupid game made up categories which only lightly touch the real subject matter of the questions. The categories simply make no sense, much like the questions. Just an opinion.

Still, we sat at the table and played into the night. Two executives at Paramount, a producer, a director, a makeup woman turned heiress and writer, a crank journalist and screenwriter, and a twelve-year-old named Aaron who doesn't like tobacco. It is worth playing Trivial Pursuit to spend time with friends in the atomized world of Hollywood. I call that a bargain. The best I ever had.

December 3, 1985

Sorry to have been out of touch. Blame it on the L.A. flu. Blame it on a one-day trip to Palm Springs. Blame it on the sickeningly smug retirees from Caterpillar tractor walking around Mission Hills Country Club with their red and yellow plaid slacks and their light blue cardigans, holding their martini glasses in their paws as they cross in front of my headlights heading toward the clubhouse.

Anyway, blame it on something that's over with, because the worm has turned.

A startling, incredible call from the studio executive who works in silk pajamas. "Listen," he said at nine this morning, "I've been thinking all the last two weeks about that story about the civil rights workers in Mississippi. Remember we told you we were going to need time to think about it?"

"Right," I said gloomily.

"We're gonna do it. I'll have Tod call your agent. It's a fabulous story. I'm glad you let me think about it for a while. I'm gonna love working on it with you."

Gasp. "That's great. I'm gonna love working on it with you, too." (Should I tell him how much I admire his silk pajama top? No. I'll just show up in one at the next meeting. The sincerest form of flattery.)

"We love working with you, Benjy. We love the story, boychick."

"I love you, too, pal."

Oh, thank God.

While I was dressing, a surprise visit from Stacey and Traci. They were both still awake from a big night on the town last night, but still going strong.

"Look," Stacey said. "We want you to know how bad we feel about what we said. The next time anyone we know tells us any of that stuff against Jews, we'll punch him."

"Thank you."

They both fixed me with bloodshot, watery twenty-two-year-old eyes. "By the way," Traci said, "we've noticed something. You're sad all the time."

"Not today."

"Yeah, but most of the time. When we first met you five years ago, you were really happy just to be you. Now you're running a race all the time trying to be all these other people, too. You're sad all the time. We want you to be happy," Traci added.

"I feel great today," I said again.

"The thing that worries me," Traci continued, "is that I'm afraid that when I get to be real old I'll be sad all the time, too. Does that happen to everyone when you get to be old?"

"Yes, Traci. Yes it does."

They both looked downcast.

"No, it doesn't. I was just kidding. None of it will ever happen to you."

"Really?" Stacey asked, hugging me.

"Really?" Traci asked, hugging me.

"For sure. Count on it. It won't ever happen to you."

Dinner at Morton's with Michael and Michelle. Michael has heard about my success as a high school teacher on the Paramount lot. "I wonder if you would have any interest in trying to develop a script for me on those same lines?" he asked as we ordered our John Dory.

"Michael, I would love to work with you on anything I could. You know I love your work."

"Well, I love your work, too," Michael said. "This is about a high school teacher dealing with a group of ninth-, tenth-, and eleventh-grade girls in a boarding school in Colorado. We need your deft touch to get at their essential vulnerability as both children and women."

"While they're discovering their bodies?"

"If you think that's appropriate," Michael said. "Casting starts anytime you say."

Craig, the new captain, had decorated the dining room to reek of festivity. There was holly everywhere. Little white and red lights. A huge tree covered with foil and stars. It was swell.

At the table next to us sat a foursome. Henry Gluck, president of Caesar's World, and his guests. *The Wall Street Journal* says he has completely turned the company around. He looked happy. I wonder where he would be eating if he had not turned Caesar's World around.

Up at the front of the room, at a little deuce, was one of the genuine gentlemen of the business. John Fiedler, a former chain-smoker and owner of Lou Von Fiedler, a dog. Also head of production at Columbia. About two years ago he left Paramount. Before that he had left Rastar. Now he's doing fine.

At the second round table, right under the huge Christmas tree, was the celebrity table of the night. Jerry Weintraub, the new head of United Artists, sat with his staff of top executives. Bob Lawrence, whom I used to see walking along the beach at Malibu deep in thought, who also used to be at Columbia, is now head of production at UA. Ken Kleinberg, a lawyer with a baby face, is now head of business affairs at UA. A long way from Civil Procedure.

Agents and producers appeared at the Weintraub table with clocklike regularity, kissing cheeks, shaking hands, slapping on the back, tummeling with power and money. Everyone at the table looked not only happy, but very, very happy.

At the first table was Roy Scheider, eating with Marty Starger, heavyweight producer, partner of Elton Rule, maker of *Mask*.

Tony Thomopoulos strolled in with an agent, slapped a few backs, and went over to the Weintraub Royal Table. He left as head of ABC a few weeks ago. No problem. Now he's at United Artists, too, laughing and scratching, having a fine time in the mud of power and money.

At the square table next to him sat Al Burton and his staggeringly beautiful wife, Sally. Al is not that important. He only invented *Facts of Life, Diff'rent Strokes, One Day At A Time, Square Pegs, Silver Spoons, Fernwood Tonight, Domestic Life,* and *Charles in Charge*.

I took a bite of my light, flaky New Zealand whitefish. Then I looked back to Michael. "How about if in the first episode, one of the ninth-grade girls is just becoming aware of the interest that boys have in her body? Does that sound right?"

"Exactly right. I love that. I think that's enough for us to have a really good start at casting. I'll call in the usual girls. Have I told you about this new one, Marcie? A very hot little item?"

"The one who does the risk arbitrage for Ivan Boesky? The one who outsmarted Boone Pickens? I don't think we need to see Marcie."

In the parking lot I waited for the Mexican valet parkers to bring up my car. It is broken, as it always is. The brakes make a terrifying sound. The car stops, but I get scared. Especially when I'm going downhill.

J. and B., major agents, walked out and shook my hand. "How you doin', buddy?" I asked B. "Everything all right?"

("Everything all right?" is the standard Hollywood greeting this year. It absolutely precludes any answer except, "Great. Everything all right with you?")

"Everything's great," B. said. "Everything all right with you?"

"Just great."

"Listen, you won't believe what I've done," B. said. "I've gotten a bidding war going for *The Brothers Karamazov*. Between Tom at Paramount and Larry at MGM."

"You're kidding. You maniac."

"No, I boiled it down. I told them, it's a story about a father and a son both in love with a really hot bitch. The father is murdered. After that, it's a courtroom drama about whether the son did it. Both Tom and Larry jumped for it."

"Great," I said. "Do you think you can get Dostoevsky to do the script?"

B. winked at me. "That's what Larry at MGM asked me, too."

DECEMBER 6, 1985

Another big day. First, a meeting at the studio with my fellow producer, Schmuel, two studio executives, Tom and Doug, and their secretary, Judy, to go over a "writers' list." The idea is that we will first have a menu of studio-approved writers. Then we will choose the one we like best and hire him or her to write our script about the three slain civil rights workers.

My partner, Schmuel, is an interesting guy. His parents were prisoners in Dachau, and then they were prisoners in Siberia. Somehow they got to Israel. Schmooey himself was a paratrooper in the Israeli army. He fought on the Golan Heights in 1967 and 1973. He is terrifyingly matter-of-fact.

I wish you could have seen our list. I wish you could have been in the room.

"What about Bo Goldman? You think he's good enough?" Schmooey asked.

"I like him," I said. "I loved *Melvin and Howard*."

"Yes," Tom, the studio executive said. "But if we got Larry Kasdan, we'd have both the writer and the director right off the bat."

"Well, I liked *The Big Chill*. Larry Kasdan would be fine," I said.

"No," Schmooey said. "Larry Kasdan will only do his own material. What do you think about Paul Brickman? He's another writer-director."

"Well, *Risky Business* was great," Tom said. "But I hear his price for a draft and a set is a million dollars."

"I think if he wants to do it, we should pay him the million and be happy," Schmooey said.

"How about Tom Benedek?" Doug asked. "Anybody like him?"

"I thought *Cocoon* had no real ending," I said. "Otherwise he's great."

"I agree," Schmooey added grimly.

"What about Tom Rickman?" I put in.

"I hear his price is up to three hundred thousand for a draft," Doug said.

"If we have to spend it, we have to spend it," Schmooey said. "But I hear he's doing only his own ideas."

"No, he takes assignments," Tom answered. "Let's talk to him."

"How about Bob Towne?" Doug asked.

"Well, everyone loved *Chinatown*," Schmooey said. "But he takes three years to turn in a script."

"Plus, his price is a million dollars for a draft," Tom said. "I think that's a little high."

Finally we made a list of our top ten writer candidates and agreed to start "accessing" their agents to see if they would do us the favor of considering writing our script for a price that almost surely will not be less than four thousand dollars *per page*.

The joke is that this morning, in and around Burbank, Studio City, Hollywood, Beverly Hills, and Culver City, there were probably fifty meetings about "comedies with heart." Probably the exact same group of writers is being discussed at every single meeting. Beginning a meeting by talking about getting Bo Goldman or Larry Kasdan is sort of like starting out a visit with your doctor by saying, "Assume that I'm going to live forever. . . ." It has the same quality of realism.

Still, I love the insiderliness of it. The very fact that it is being done everywhere else in town means we're all in the club.

As we started to leave, Schmooey took Tom aside and whispered to him. Tom nodded.

In the parking lot I asked Schmooey what he had been talking about.

"Oh, nothing," he said irritably. "I just told him that because I have more experience with producing than you do, I would be the producer and you would have some very nice title like executive producer."

"What the hell are you talking about? It was my idea. It was my pitch that sold the goddamned thing. No way, unless executive producer gets paid more than you do."

Schmooey looked at me with pity. "Ben, Ben, Ben," he said. "Why do you take all this so personally? We already had this conversation a long time ago. You agreed I would be in charge."

"No way, pal. We're partners or there's nothing going on. Period."

I was glad he was not holding an Uzi. He looked deeply distraught. Perhaps angry. I'd rather not think he was actually angry. We stared at each other for a few seconds. "All right," he said. "We tell our lawyers to work it out."

Who cares anyway? In my rearview mirror later today on the way home I saw the sun setting at the end of Sunset Boulevard. The sky was blue and pink and gray. The wind was blowing palm fronds high into the air. Swallows were soaring behind the pink cupolas of the Beverly Hills Hotel. Two rows of royal palms marched off toward the ocean with the orange sun falling between them. I saw all of this in my rearview mirror, not in a movie, but in real life.

December 7, 1985

Dinner with my pal Rich Procter at Spago. Alex did not feel like going out. She wears braces. She is thirty-eight. When the orthodontist, Dr. Loberg, tightens the braces, she is in agony. Dr. Loberg tightened the braces yesterday, so Alex is in agony, lying in the dark at home wishing she had never gotten braces. "You got them so your teeth would be perfect, like the rest of you," I always tell her.

"Yeah, right," she always says.

Neither of us likes to talk about not having children any longer, so she lay in the dark and I went to Spago with Rich Procter.

Rich had a great idea for a funny movie. "It's like this," he said. "Suppose that Shakespeare was broke and desperately needed to write something to make money."

"Yeah?"

"And so he comes up with an idea for *Romeo and Juliet, Part Two*. In this one, Juliet's father puts her in a convent for wayward girls, and they're all comparing their bodies when Romeo comes in dressed like a nun. Then Romeo's discovered, and they're going to kill him, but instead he gets put in the Venetian army, only he's not really an army type, and he has a lot of wacky adventures in the army, and then finally he meets Juliet again in Malta, and they're happy until a Moor with a chainsaw appears. . . ."

Rich is a funny guy. "The only problem with it is that it's too original," I told him, and it's true. Hollywood values doing the old formulas dead-on perfect. It does not like new formulas. See for yourself.

On the way out I ran into Brandon Tartikoff. "A true hero," I said to him. Brandon is the head of programming at NBC. "You've done incredible work, pal. I love *Miami Vice*."

"Yes, we got lucky, Ben," he said. "I hear next week's is even better."

The best part of the evening was that he remembered my name. I can't even remember where we met. I guess that shows he's a smart guy and I'm a superficial guy. I wish it were true. Maybe it is.

(No, I'm just kidding. It's not true at all. You'll see.)

December 10, 1985

F. Scott Fitzgerald said that when the Dutch sailors first looked over the gunwales and saw Long Island, then saw that a huge, forested, endless continent loomed behind the island, for the first time man saw something commensurate with the power of his imagination. To me, that has always been the best description of America. It is a place in the imagination, without limits or fixed poles, any more than imagination has limits.

I thought of that passage in *The Great Gatsby* over and over for the past few days.

On Saturday, my genius friend Sheryl (who graduated from Princeton summa cum laude in three years and dresses like Madonna) and I saw *Spies Like Us*. I had a small role in creating that movie, and I had mostly been deprived of credit and money. Still, the movie had clever touches—the foreign-service types pushing cookies across a silver salver as a nuclear warhead approaches, a Russian missile crew listening to a bad rock 'n' roll song, "Soulfinger." It had sweeping vistas in Siberia and camel chases in Afghanistan. I felt as if I had been on a perfect trip into another place, both safe and dangerous in my two hours at the Mann's Bruin.

On Sunday afternoon I saw *Young Sherlock Holmes*. Let's not mince words about that one. It is spectacularly good. The sets, characters, dialogue, plot, everything that makes a drama, carried me away from Westwood, with its littered streets, and into the orderly but sinister world of the Brompton School, London W.l, circa 1890. Sadly, Spielberg felt bound to steal an entire long sequence about crazed Orientals sacrificing maidens from his own *Indiana Jones*. But otherwise the story was pure gold. I was on the edge of my seat for a solid hour wondering how Sherlock and Watson would get out alive. In the dark, far in the back, I enjoyed my two hours in London on Westwood Boulevard far more than I have ever enjoyed London on Park Row or Sloane Square.

Tonight I saw *Rocky IV*. There were virtually no other customers. The story is shockingly contrived, and the dialogue absolutely bankrupt. But there was one incredibly evocative scene. Dolph Lundgren plays a mountain of a Soviet boxer. He comes to Las Vegas to fight Rocky's old pal, Apollo Creed.

As Dolph Lundgren gets into the ring, suddenly the ring rises through the roof into the main auditorium-coliseum of the MGM Grand. The Soviet boxer cannot believe his eyes. There are hundreds of beautiful showgirls dancing eerily, lasciviously to the music of James Brown. There are two airplanes flying through the sky inside the huge room. There are spangles and spotlights and jewels and legs and breasts and money and opulence and decadence everywhere. The Russian is simply struck dumb by the vision of capitalist heaven that appears as he rises through what he thought was the ceiling of a man's experience and expectations.

(Lundgren as the Soviet, of course, was seeing nothing less than *the movies* shaping life.)

In the deserted Studio City theater, I watched Rocky and Lundgren battle it out for decency, country, and what a man's gotta do. I knew it was pure corn. I knew it was manipulation. But I leaped up and cheered, I threw my popcorn at the screen, I screamed when Rocky knocked out that brute who had wantonly killed his best friend.

For twenty minutes in the ring, I was bigger, stronger, braver, tougher than I will ever be in my life. I was Rocky, and it felt great.

Movies are that way. In a way which is never even approached by painting or sculpture or ballet (except for ballet music), they reach into our imaginations and remake us from our imaginations out. They change our lives, our perspectives, our hopes, who we want to be. They have a power as great as human imagination, like the power of the idea of America.

I often think that it is not in any way coincidence that movies are a peculiarly American art form, and especially not a coincidence that they come from L.A.

The American frontier ended on the ground when the pioneers and the Hawkeyes reached the Pacific Ocean. But Americans needed a frontier, a place beyond the reach of convention and the ordinary. By a miracle of technological coincidence, the frontier went up onto a screen almost immediately after the terra firma frontier closed.

Movies are that promised land where a man can stand straighter and taller, braver, handsomer, and richer than he ever could in a sweatshop in Passaic. Up on that rayon acetate screen a woman is more beautiful, sexier, more clever, more likely to run a plantation with her delicate hands and then be swept upstairs by Rhett Butler so that he can have his way with her, than she ever would be washing dishes in Oak Park. The Bijou is where powerless, lonely, frightened children can throw off all of the terror of childhood and instead move to its secret rhythm of excitement, mystery, and danger. I thought these thoughts as I drove past the male hookers on Ventura and the swinging singles in front of Sasch. There was an uncharacteristic cold wind blowing across the Valley and just starting its way up the hills to our house. The billboards for Las Vegas shook and shivered in the wind.

To think that this mental edifice is built by gaffers and sound men and boom men and carpenters and electricians in very large part. Those same men might have built a strip shopping center which would vanish into no one's unconscious and a few men's tax-loss accounting. But they chose to build a cathedral of human possibility which will be in someone's dreams for as long as there is someone.

It made me shake with excitement in my freezing cold car. I am only a tiny player in the game. I have been beating my brains out against a cement wall here for ten years when I had lifetime job security in the East. But that was a job. My work here, sporadic as it is, is pioneering on the frontier. In a small way, but still in a way, I am part of the enterprise which builds commensurate with man's imagination.

It all made me happy. When I got up to Mulholland, I could see that the wind had driven the smog far out toward Hawaii. The basin was clear, dazzling with lights, a powerhouse of human beings wanting to meld into imagination. It's home.

DECEMBER 11, 1985

Back to the carbon monoxide on Sunset Boulevard, far below the nighttime lights of the city or the sailors spying an endless continent. Back to reality.

A meeting with David M., a "creative executive" at Paramount. David M. is a neat, bearded man with a fidgety air. "How the hell have you been, pal?" he asked. "How come you never come in to pitch me stories anymore?"

"I'm sorry, my man. I've been busy. Really. But I'm gonna make up for it today. I have some great stories."

"Go for it, pal."

"Okay. First. There's this fantastically rich entrepreneur. He's a corporate looter. He buys this textile factory in South Carolina. It's a monster with company-owned housing for the whole labor force. The looter gets the workers to buy their own houses, and they all go into debt. Then the fucker closes the factory and the workers are ruined. Two of them come to L.A. to try to get the bastard to change his mind. He has them beaten up and arrested.

They're pissed off. The two guys are going back to Carolina when suddenly they get an idea. They're gonna sting this rich guy like in *The Sting* and completely ruin his life and take away all his money. And they get together with his ex-wife and do it."

David M. stroked his beard and nodded vigorously a few times. "It's all there," he said. "Definitely all there. It's not fantastic, but the whole story's there. You thinking of any writers?"

"Yeah, I was thinking of Peter Hankoff. I like him."

"He's fine. Is he interested?"

"Oh, definitely."

"All right. The two of you have a talk and then see if you can work anything out, and then come see me and we'll see if Dawn likes it."

"Great."

"What else do you have?"

"Okay. You know how in New York there are these guys who play three-card monte on the street corners, and there's no way you can ever beat 'em?"

"Right."

"Well, now they have these same streety-looking black guys with their furry little hats and they're hustling these white-bread commuters who get off the trains from Connecticut, only they're playing chess. And these black dudes get five tables set up and they play chess with five investment bankers at a time, and they beat them all."

"So?"

"So, imagine that one of them is Eddie Murphy, and he's picked up by a white guy in a Paul Stuart suit who turns out to be from the CIA, and they put Eddie Murphy into a chess tournament in Russia, only really he's a spy, and he's got a mission. . . ."

I trailed off because I could see David M. covering his lips with his finger. That is an unconscious signal that he—or any other listener—does not really want to hear any more.

"What's wrong?" I asked.

"The problem is that Eddie Murphy playing chess is what

makes that story unique, but Eddie Murphy playing chess just isn't visual enough."

"Okay. You're right. I didn't see it, but you're right.

"Okay. Here's another one. Try this. There's this guy at a kind of seedy collection agency on a side street in Washington. The guy is a washed-up detective and he's just sitting there reading the *Post* sports page when suddenly a neatly dressed bureaucrat strolls in and says, 'I'd like for you to collect some money for us. A bad debt.' And the seedy detective says, 'Okay, but I usually get thirty percent of whatever I collect.'

"So the bureaucrat says okay, and the detective asks what the deal is. The bureaucrat says he's from the World Bank, and there's this little country called Boca Grande that owes us four billion dollars. Go down there and see how much of it you can get. . . ."

David M. began to nod vigorously and to shake his head and then to nod again. "I can see that one," he said. "It has possibilities."

"Sort of like *The In-Laws* only with more spin," I said.

"Writers?"

"The only guy who could do it right is this amazing, creative guy named Rich Procter, who told me the story in the first place," I said.

"Okay, get me a script by him and we'll see where we are," David M. said.

"Good, you'll love his script. *Destroy All Teenagers*. It's hilarious."

"What else have you got?"

"How about this. There's this real fancy English public school, like Eton or Harrow. And it's supposed to have an exchange program with these kids from a really snooty private school in Highland Park, near Dallas. Only the guys at the Education Ministry get confused and send the forms to a high school in Highland Park, near Detroit, which is one of the all-time toughest schools in the world, right in the ghetto. So suddenly at Eton are six of the toughest, raunchiest kids you've ever seen, set against the most snotty, refined, richest English kids you'd ever want to see. . . ."

"I don't know. 'Fish out of water' may be getting a little old. Plus, *Young Sherlock* is doing absolutely no business. I don't think so."

"Okay. How about a new teenage version of *Carmen* only set in the Valley?"

David M. shook his head and ostentatiously stared at his watch.

"Hey, listen, pal, you've got a couple of pretty good items there. Let's see what you can do in the way of writers, and in a day or two we'll see where we are."

"Okay, bud. I'll call you after I've talked to Hankoff and let you know what he says. Okay?"

"Great."

I called Peter Hankoff. We set up dinner at Morton's. It was pretty cool. We sat next to Eileen Maisel, a former executive at CBS, and a writer who once worked on a project for me. I felt embarrassed to be seen with another writer. It was a slow night at Morton's.

Over crabcakes, we hammered out a story line. The high point is that the good guys from the textile factory entrap the rich guy at a love nest with a fourteen-year-old girl. Maybe the kind that you can look at, but you can't touch. Not unless you get to know her. Or buy her a Sony stereo monitor.

DECEMBER 12, 1985

I hate the fucking stock market. For a few weeks I have been carrying S & P 100 options closing out on December 20, strike price 200. This morning, I sold them. I lost about all the money I had put into them, which is typical. Still, I wrote it off as a bad bet.

I went off on my rounds. Today is my last day of seeing my

shrink, Saul. Maybe I gave you the wrong impression about him. Basically, he's about the smartest guy I know in this town, and he's got a heart as big as a Cadillac. I first started to see him because I felt suicidal about losing twenty thousand dollars in one day speculating in gold. He kept me afloat when I had a mad, hopeless crush on a gorgeous blue-eyed stewardess. He's been the padding around the walls of my cell of ambition and self-loathing.

But after five years, I'd like to try it out in the world. So I'm going on parole. I can still report in if I feel terrible, but basically I'm going to take the blows and let the record show I did it my way.

"The way we've worked it out is that I get crapped on over at Warner, and then you say, 'Come here and cry on my shoulder,' and I tell you what a great guy you are for helping me, and then you tell me what a noble, pure soul I am out in the world of those Philistines, and we both tell each other we're too good for the world of hustlers and money grubbers, and meanwhile our tongues are hanging out and we're just dying to have some of that filthy money and just hoping and praying that we could be a little less perfect and have a little more money. Right?"

"Exactly right," he said.

"Okay. I'll try it out there without the excuses for failing for just a while, and then we'll see how it goes."

He nodded and looked sad. The planes of his cheeks below his eyes sagged. His office has huge windows overlooking a street in Westwood. In the fall—and I have been five falls there—the sun throws a gauzy light through the thermo-pane glass. The leafless willow outside is cast in a spidery, weaving silhouette on the wall above Saul's leather chair and his patient face.

A willowy hula dancer is gliding on her slim hips on the beige plaster, listening to our endless sighs and whispers and then interpreting the pain with her hands, washing it out into the whistling Santa Ana wind and telling us to start anew as the willow leaves do each year.

"Would you be proud of me if I were your son, Saul?"

"I would be proud of you if I were your son," he said, and I hugged him. That's psychotherapy here in the golden land.

On the way home, I drove through Century City. The students from Beverly Hills High were pouring out in their Jaguars and Corvettes. On the radio, the CBS news told me that the stock fucking market had reached an all-time high today. Had I held on to my options I would have made a thousand dollars today. Instead, I lost about a thousand dollars. I hate the stock market. It makes me feel small.

DECEMBER 13, 1985

A big night.

Dinner at Morton's with Alex and with Josh, a lawyer at Paramount, and his wife, the mousy but sexy Susan. At the big round table next to us were a dozen major hitters: Dick Zanuck and his wife, Lily. Sherry Lansing and her pal, Wayne Rogers. Irwin Winkler, as in *Rocky* Chartoff-Winkler. Alan *Star Wars* Ladd, Jr. Ron Howard. Heavy-duty chiefs here in Hollywood.

The restaurant was packed with prosperous, excited men and women, which is rare for a Friday night. Usually, Friday night is "schmata night," so named for the wealthy people from Encino who manufacture garments and money. Those people are generally prosperous, but not excited. Anyway, tonight was a big night for showbiz and schmata-biz folks, drinking vodka and tonics, milling at the bar, shouting out orders to waiters and busboys.

We sat at our table, eating our crabcakes, when suddenly there was a commotion next to us. Dick Zanuck was getting up to go to the bathroom as he had been doing all night. A man from the garment business kept getting jostled by the feisty producer.

The commotion started because the man told Zanuck to cut it the fuck out and stop bothering them. Zanuck, without a moment's warning that I could see, swung on the garmento and broke his nose in one swift punch. Blood poured out everywhere. The waiters made a flying wedge to keep the two combatants apart. The captain hustled the victim, broken nose and blood and all, to the men's room, slapping on towels and ice as they ran.

Dick Zanuck looked very happy with himself. He went back to his table and smiled, then had another drink.

The man with the broken nose was with a large angry woman. The woman turned out to be a personal injury lawyer. She called the cops.

Just as Dick Zanuck was blowing out the candles on his birthday cake, two of the Los Angeles County Sheriff's Department's finest appeared at the door. The sight of those two men, in their green nylon jackets, with their nightsticks and their .38s at the ready in their holsters, peering into the maw of Morton's, was a jewel. The closest I could give you was a mixture of awe and fury and disgust. It reminded me of the look on Dolph Lundgren's face when he comes up through the floor into the MGM Grand in *Rocky IV*. It's pretty overwhelming, but the cops are going to have the last laugh. So I thought.

Craig, the maître d', discreetly summoned Dick Zanuck to talk to the cops. He walked out, a sprightly gamecock, with the restaurant's eyes on him. Outside, on the brick, trellised patio between the restaurant and the parking lot, Dick Zanuck patiently explained his side of the story. The policemen looked at first contemptuous, then skeptical, then neutral, then friendly. Maybe they had not recognized the name at first.

One of them started to write out a fairly harmless citation maybe for assault and battery. He went into the kitchen looking for the victim to swear out a complaint. The victim came rushing out, a towel to his nose. "You wanna complaint," he shouted. "I'll give you a complaint. . . ." The cops took him outside as well and talked to him patiently for a few minutes while Dick Zanuck hovered calmly inside the restaurant.

In a few more minutes, the "complainant" got into his car and drove away, without signing a complaint. Fantastic.

Dick Zanuck walked over to his celebrity table, then gave a little bow. Sherry and Ron and Irwin and Wayne and Lily and Alan burst into applause.

I guess they were thinking about how blood will tell. They were probably thinking how they had totally outclassed everyone around them, dazzled the police, and shown why the top dogs are on top. I kept thinking that if Dick Zanuck had been one of the parking lot attendants up from Chihuahua, he would already be in jail. "To him who hath shall be given" is the name of that song.

Diners, drinkers, waiters, busboys, everyone in the room was thoroughly jazzed by that time. There was a rapid, strained, jerky quality to people's speech, to their motions, even to the way they flicked their eyes around the room. It all reminded me of *The Damned*, so we left.

I took Alex home and sat her in front of the TV, where Don Johnson and Philip Michael Thomas were arresting a group of women cocaine dealers. They were supposed to look hard and tough. In fact, I think they looked a lot friendlier than most of the women at Trump's.

I had a late date. Late in every way. Jack Jacobson, the principal of Birmingham High School, my new home, had invited me to the "Winter Wonderland Vice Versa Dance" at Birmingham High. It was supposed to end at eleven-thirty. If I drove fast I could be there by eleven-fifteen. When I got there, the parking lot was virtually empty. A damp, cold wind was blowing off the Sepulveda Basin. A few teacher-guard-chaperons stopped me on my way into the "multipurpose room." I told them who I was, and they nodded to let me in.

The room had a disc jockey playing a rock version of the theme from *Miami Vice*. There was a revolving glittering sphere throwing light all around. There were five or six couples dancing a no-touching dance in the center of the room next to a decorated Christmas tree.

Mr. Orear, the vice principal, walked over to me. "You're late," he said. "They chose the 'most eligible male' at ten-thirty and then almost everyone left."

"I'm sorry I missed that," I said. "I was watching a fight."

Jeff Lippmann, a very smart kid who sits near me in U.S. Government, walked over. "Hi, Mr. Stein," he said. He introduced his girlfriend, a shy, pretty Chinese girl named Clara. "Hi, Mr. Stein," she said. "I saw you in Advanced English class."

I stood alone for a few minutes in the room. It was dim, unlit except by the lights of the Christmas tree and the light coming in from the hall. In the quarter light, I could not clearly make out any faces. For all I knew they were the faces of Neely Holmead or Jim Thompson or Joel Block or Susan Jacobs back at Montgomery Blair High School in Silver Spring, Maryland, in 1961. Without any effort at all, I was back in the boys' gym at the Christmas dance with Bunny Serbin. The eternal, classic perfection of that room as the Platonic situs of high school dances of all time sucked me into its maw. I was almost hallucinating, and the hallucination was that if I could only stay in that room, that dim, almost empty room far out in the San Fernando Valley for all time, I would be young for all time. The gravitational field of wanting to be young was overwhelming, irresistible.

This is it, I thought as the record shifted to Phil Collins. *I've finally lost my mind, and now I'm crazy for the rest of my life, fantasying that I'm a high school student. Perfect.*

The youth room was drawing all the reality out of my mind like a lancet drawing blood. *I'm going to have to write a note to Joan Didion about the real meaning of "vertiginous occlusion,"* I thought, and then suddenly the spell was broken.

I walked back through the room, said good night to Jeff and Clara, and ventured out into the cold and damp night.

On the way home, along the freeway, I still felt dazed, alarmed, frightened by my own agony about youth. Oh, you fools at Morton's, thinking you have everything worthwhile with your cars and your money and your deals. The only real value is youth, the only meaningful coin of life, and you and I can only watch the truly rich of the world, the young, as they frisk on the beach and at the Winter Wonderland Dance.

December 14, 1985

Tonight was Peter Morton's black tie Christmas party—by very exclusive invitation only—at Morton's.

It was the kind of event where you start a conversation with Steve Tisch, and after a few minutes he says, "Well, it's like what Uncle Larry said when he took over CBS. . . ."

There were the usual suspects—Mark Canton, president of Warner; John Fiedler, head of production at Columbia, who told us that he had been denied visiting rights to his dog, Lou Von Fiedler; Ted Kotcheff, who told us about his problems filming *Uncommon Valor;* Tony Yerkovich, who gets only a "created by" credit on each and every episode of *Miami Vice*, who wants us to invest in a club he is starting in Venice; Bess Armstrong, who looked great; Joan Collins, who wore the most dazzling diamond necklace I have ever seen, borrowed, some say, from Fred for the evening; Allan Carr, looking relatively slim; and Jon *Risky Business* Avnet, who complained about the janitorial service in his office at Paramount.

Alex and I sat with Garth Wood, a genuinely original English shrink, obviously rolling in dough, an Old Harrovian who divides his time between London and Palm Beach, and his wife, Pat, a photographer, model, and novelist. Pat has a book out called *Palm Beach*, which has its own promotion right on the cover. If you buy the book you get a coupon. The coupon enters you in a contest to win a free trip to Palm Beach.

"I thought of it myself," she said. "Pretty sharp, eh?"

DECEMBER 16, 1985

Back to the daily details of life in Los Angeles. My assistant, Sara, drove me over to Merlin Olsen Porsche to pick up the goddamned car. The brakes are broken again. A mere five hundred bucks. *God, I hate that car.*

On the way over we fell into conversation about history.

"My birthday is on Lincoln's Birthday," she said. "Did you know that?"

"No," I answered. "Do you know what great national event Abraham Lincoln presided over?"

"I sure do," Sara said. "The Gettysburg Address."

"No, I mean what great national catastrophe."

"The Gettysburg Address."

"No, I mean more like what was the event of which the Gettysburg Address was a small incident?"

Sara looked bewildered. "Give me a hint."

"It was a war."

"The Vietnam war."

"No, not the Vietnam war."

"Then I don't know."

"The Civil War. Abraham Lincoln was president during the Civil War. His election precipitated the Civil War."

"When was that?" Sara asked suspiciously, as if I might be making it up.

"Well, when was the Civil War?"

"I don't know."

"Well, it was about eighty-seven years after the founding of this country. How old is the United States of America?"

"Thirty years?"

I looked off in the distance toward the San Bernardino

Mountains. It wouldn't be so bad if Sara were not planning to be first a hair model and then a surgeon, but she is.

"The United States of America is about two hundred and ten years old. The Civil War ran from 1861 to 1865. It was a great national tragedy. There were close to a million killed on both sides."

"I can't believe I didn't know that," Sara sighed. "I'm really good in history."

DECEMBER 17, 1985

A pitch meeting at Paramount with Tamara Rawitt, the head of Eddie Murphy Productions. The weather has changed completely. It is now sunny, dry, and hot.

Tamara has her office where Joel *"Commando"* Silver used to have his office. It is right next to Bob Wachs's office, where Larry Gordon, currently president of Fox production, once had his office. I pitched along with Rich Procter, my brilliant friend.

"First, I have this idea about a guy who runs a two-bit collection office in Washington, D.C. One day a very neatly dressed man from the World Bank comes to see him. The guy from the bank tells him that the bank wants him to collect a debt. The collections guy, that's Eddie Murphy, says he usually gets fifty percent of whatever he collects. So the bureaucrat tells Eddie Murphy that this Central American country, Boca Grande, owes the International Monetary Fund three billion dollars, and Eddie Murphy can keep half of anything he can get. So off they go. . . ."

"I kind of like it," Tamara said.

"Right, so Eddie Murphy finds an old pink Cadillac that had belonged to the last dictator, and he takes it apart and finds thirty million dollars in it, but then he meets some really poor villagers and he gives them the money and comes home empty-handed and goes back to his little office."

"I like it a lot." Tamara nodded. "What else do you have?"

Rich Procter said, "Well, this is just my own idea, but how about Eddie Murphy is just getting out of the service and he comes to a bar in Washington, and someone poisons him with a really slow-acting poison, and a doctor tells him he only has a week to live, and Eddie has to run all around D.C. trying to find out what the hell happened. It's sort of like a combination of *48 Hrs.* and *Beverly Hills Cop*, because he's up against the Washington establishment and he has a deadline."

"I love that, and I'm gonna try to sell that thing. I really love that. I'll call you next week."

Rich and I went out into the hot sun in front of the main administration building feeling as if we were kings. It's a delusion, but everything good in Hollywood is a delusion. That's why they call it Hollywood.

We ate lunch in the Paramount Commissary. It's a light, airy room with a lot of windows and French doors and white art-deco latticework. We sat at a table and watched the whole world drift by. George Wendt and Ted Danson from *Cheers* drifted in. Carl Reiner ate salad with Steve Martin. We ate turkey and wondered if Tamara could get us a deal.

On the way out, I saw a diminutive, good-looking young man sitting on the stoop eating with a pretty girl. "Hi, Mr. Stein," Michael J. Fox said. "I love your column. I loved that one where you said that Lea Thompson was your absolute favorite actress."

"Thank you," I said. "She is good. She was just in a big picture this summer. What the hell was that?"

"I think maybe it was my picture *Back to the Future*," Michael Fox said in a soft voice.

December 18, 1985

And speaking of children . . .

A morning at Birmingham High School. Our teacher looked particularly fetching in a youthful hairdo. She was making out progress reports and the class was "relaxing" as she put it.

The usual knot of precocious teenagers, almost all boys, gathered around me and I asked them what they wanted to do with their lives.

"Make money," came the chorus.

"Like, I'd like to go to school and become a CPA and then go to law school and become a tax lawyer, because helping people not pay tax is where the real money is," said one smart boy with a small beard.

"International banking," said another boy. "Banking is cool. Big bucks."

"Maybe owning a hospital," another said. "Hospitals manufacture money."

"I can't believe this," I said. "Is there any one of you who wants to do something even though there's no money in it?"

The boy who wanted to be a tax lawyer scratched his chin. "Yes, there's this girl who wanted to be a doctor in Ethiopia, but," he added proudly, "I think I talked her out of it."

"You talked her out of it! Why?"

"Because why should she go to school all those years and then come out of school with debts and then go work for people who won't even have any money to pay her?"

I stared at the kids. They stared back. I stared more. They blinked.

"Well," a girl next to me said, "really, what counts is doing something you like doing, something you're proud of."

"Yeah, and I'd like to have a family that really loved me," the boy with the beard said. "That comes before money."

"I don't even think you can measure anything in terms of money except money," said another boy. "You have to be proud of yourself."

"Mr. Stein," said the boy with the beard, "you have to come out on a Saturday night with us. We go crazy. We go to an ice cream place and eat whipped cream and spit it at each other."

I love being around children. They want so much to please. They want to be cool, and to be smart, and to be idealistic, and to be daring, and to be clever and to be stupid, all at once.

After class I walked across the campus and watched the children eating lunch. The sun was dazzling on their small, unlined faces. I felt as if I could inhale the essence of youth just by being in the same room with them, just by being on the same grounds with them. When I go out to Birmingham these days, the hardest part of each day is leaving, and going back to work.

When I got home, Traci, one of my ex-Valley Girls, was waiting for me. She flopped around our bedroom like a tall, beautiful, confused crane. "I started work today at a job," she said. "And I walked into the room, and it was like a mortuary. I was the youngest person in there by twenty years. And all I would have been doing all day is sitting at a desk reading a newspaper to make sure everything was on the financial page. And it struck me that no one ever laughed, or raised his voice, and it was like being buried. So I went to the ladies' room and I started to cry. And I told them I felt sick, and I went home. And when I was in my car, I just started tearing off my business suit and tossed my briefcase in the back seat and I was out in the sunshine and I started to sing. I was so happy I wasn't in that office, I felt like I had just gotten out of the hospital. Like I had just been born."

She jumped off the bed, jumped on the bed again, walked around, picked up Martha, the Weimaraner, like a matchstick, and set her down, then ran out to the pool and twirled around and around in the sun.

DECEMBER 19, 1985

Our teacher was sweet today. She helped the class plan their schedules, write out college applications, and figure out financial aid charts. To reward her, I offered her a prize: dinner, with me, at Spago.

Alex never goes out anymore. She stays in bed reading one mystery novel every four hours, then sleeping for another four hours, then reading another mystery novel. Very rarely, she varies the routine by watching our sacred videotape of *Gone with the Wind*. Of course, that's her routine when she has the flu, which she only has some of the time. The L.A. flu. Brought here by the Mongol hordes. As hard to get rid of as greed or envy.

I told Alex I would bring her back a duck sausage pizza (and I did).

At Spago, the teacher was already waiting. She could not wait to tell me that she is planning to run for Congress next year. "I only have a couple of problems," she said. "First, I don't have a cent."

"Well, don't worry about that," I said. "Politics doesn't cost anything."

"Second," she said, "I don't live in the district I'm planning to run from, and I've never lived in it. And third, I'm not a member of the United Teachers of Los Angeles, who are the only people who might even conceivably want to support me with real money."

"I see."

"On the other hand, I've almost never tried for anything and failed. In fact, when I ran for student body president in eighth grade, I lost, and my mother said, 'Honey, it's really good that you lost, because it's high time you realized you can't get everything you want.'"

"Well, I'm going to be following all of this very closely, and I hope you win. Who're you running against?"

"Bobbi Fiedler," she said, naming merely the most skillful, well-liked, well-financed candidate in the history of the San Fernando Valley, a nearly invincible name in Los Angeles politics. "I'm dying to run against her."

"And she's dying to run against you." I smiled, as we turned to our angel-hair pasta.

Peter Bogdanovich walked through the door with John Goldwyn (yes, from those Goldwyns) and a gorgeous blond woman (his wife). Peter had been in the *Los Angeles Times* this morning because he had just filed for personal bankruptcy. He had debts of something like six million dollars and assets of something under forty dollars. He blamed it all on the death of Dorothy Stratten.

John Goldwyn came rushing over to see me. "Listen, I hear you were sitting at the table with Dick Zanuck last Friday and broke up the fight. Pretty good work."

"I wasn't even at the table," I said. "I was just sitting near them. I reported the story. I wasn't in the fight."

John Goldwyn nodded sagely. "You did good," he said, and patted me on the back.

An elderly man at the table next to me grasped my wrist. He was with an elderly woman who had obviously had the most expensive boob job in history. Her face was lined and tired, but her breasts would have made any *Playboy* centerfold envious.

"You had a fight with Dick Zanuck?" he asked eagerly. "I've known the little pisher since he was born. You should have put a knife in his ribs."

"I don't even know Dick Zanuck," I said. "I just happened to be sitting nearby."

The man nodded vigorously. "The kid has less imagination in his whole body than Darryl had in his toes. But you know him better than I do, so you know that already."

"Right," I said. "Exactly."

The wife with the plastic chest winked at me.

On the way out, one of the bartenders gestured toward me.

"Nice work," he whispered over the counter. "I've been wanting to punch out that guy myself."

I shrugged. "Someone had to do it," I said, and walked out the door.

DECEMBER 20, 1985

Litigation. I spend half my life talking to lawyers.

A call this morning from the studio that bought the civil rights project. They're waffling. But they already said we had a deal. A call to my lawyer to see what's what.

Last week we had tile laid in the second bedroom. The tile man apparently washed the tiles with a mixture of gasoline and paint thinner. The room has been uninhabitable since. It's costing a thousand bucks to have the smell and the tile taken out. That's another fucking lawsuit.

This does not count the hearing and struggle against the capitalists before the Securities and Exchange Commission or a long-simmering dispute with a network about a project of mine on which they refuse to give me the contractually mandated credit.

I need an open line to Century City to talk to Marty, my lawyer. Injunctions, restraining orders, RICO, punitive damages, that's all I hear all day.

Twelve years ago, I practiced law. I hated it. I certainly did not expect that writing in Hollywood was so much about litigation and so little about imagination. But getting anything done here means either a lawsuit or the threat of a lawsuit.

Very few people here do anything because it's right. Executives at NBC or Paramount or United Artists do things because someone's standing over their heads with a club, and in my case, that someone is a lawyer.

I hate that way of life. I came here to dream, not to fight.

Maybe that's why I've never really fit in here. This is a town of street fighters, not daydreamers. But I don't know where the town of daydreamers is located. When I learn, I'll tell you.

DECEMBER 21, 1985

Surprise! Alex is feeling better. In fact, she felt so much better this morning that she decided to go to Arkansas to see her parents for Christmas. Why not? She deserves a break, and what better place to have it than at Heber Springs, Arkansas? It is a small resort north of Little Rock where Alex's parents live in a condominium near a lake. There are forests and gray skies and a place called The Red Apple Inn with waiters with little leather bow ties.

I took Alex to the Burbank airport and watched her fly away. My personal take on the subject is that Alex is an angel sent from heaven. She never acts meanly, never takes revenge, never holds a grudge. She cries when she sees homeless dogs near the freeway. She never gossips, never backbites against the losing powers at the studio. She is an angel. But angels are not humans. They cannot have children the way welfare mothers and stenographers and interior decorators can. That's what I expect to find out when I die: that Alex was an angel after all.

We've been together now for almost twenty years, ever since I saw her across a crowded reception room at the State Department on C Street at the July 4, 1966, Junior Foreign Service Officers' Ball. I thought she was a hillbilly secretary. In fact, she was a sophomore at Vassar College. Off and on, we have been the main player in each other's lives through law school, Ho, Ho, Ho Chi Minh, NLF is gonna win, through lying down on K Street to block traffic and protest the war, through separation and divorce over her absences and my cute little students, and back together again in Hollywood, far from the State Department reception room.

We can read each other's thoughts by now, and we usually spend our time together pretending to be dogs. But at the bottom line, she is an angel. Now she's off to Heber Springs.

After Alex left I came home and read to Martha, Trixie, and Ginger for an hour. Then I slept.

Then a party at the home of Tom Hoberman, my former lawyer, a power in the powerful law firm of Ziffren, Brittenham & Gullen. Tom and Ellen have a little palace on Coldwater Canyon Boulevard. Ken Ziffren greeted me at the door. "I'm sorry I haven't returned your call," he said.

"No problem." I cannot even remember why I called him, truth to tell.

I greeted a knot of pals who were lined up to visit with a psychic seated on a couch in the living room. An agent, a lawyer, another agent, a studio executive.

Out by the pool I sat next to an attractive woman in a white muumuu. "I'm a psychotherapist," she said. "I'm working on the psychological correlates of death."

"What does that mean?"

"I mean the psychological states that accompany imminent death," she explained. "Like how people feel after they've had terrible accidents."

"Very good," I said. "Nice talking to you. Maybe someday we'll talk more and I'll write an article about your research."

"Oh, heavens," she said. "If you did that, I would be apoplectic."

Go fuck yourself, I thought. One of the hallmarks of the truly stupid is that when you offer to do them a favor, they complain about it. A good table at Morton's? "I can't stand the noise." An introduction to Norman Lear? "Oh, I'm too busy playing golf." The sure mark of the loser: treating a gift as a burden.

In the dining room I picked at the desserts and talked to P., a studio executive at Paramount. "It's been a terrible weekend," he said. *"The Color Purple* opened at a third of what they expected.

Out of Africa won't make back its prints and advertising. The whole fucking system is collapsing. I give it about three months, and then every executive in town except for Mark Canton at Warner is going to get fired."

I kissed the hostess goodbye and drove away. This has been a disastrous Christmas and a disastrous year. Jack Valenti just said that if the trend continues, by next year theatrical release will be ancillary to cassettes. Nothing worked this year except *Rambo, Back to the Future, Jagged Edge,* and *Rocky IV.*

Just my chance! If I can think of the greatest story line ever created and get it made as a movie, I'll be the hero of the business. A true sweetheart of the industry. Why not? I live in dreams anyway, so why not dream a big one?

Insane with delusion, I drove down La Cienega Boulevard to Star Strip, a strip club right next to the new Ma Maison Hotel. It was perfect for L.A. The waitresses serve only fruit juices and Perrier. No alcohol. The strippers introduce themselves and smile before each number. "Hi, I'm Lana, and I'm going to dance for you. . . ."

I watched for a while and then I drove home. Why not? Why the hell not? A little kid from outer space is accused of murdering a stripper and has to be saved from a lynch mob of communists by a machine-gun-toting boxer. Why not? Yeah? Well, if you're so fucking smart, why don't you think of a better one?

DECEMBER 22, 1985

Lunch at the Hard Rock Cafe with my friend H., the studio executive who monitors *Miami Vice*. The Hard Rock is a huge restaurant-bar in the Beverly Center. It is to teen lust what Kuwait is to oil: an awful lot of it in a very small place, and major money moving in and around it.

"It looks awfully good on the screen," H. told me, "but we're having mucho trouble with it."

We both ate spare ribs and looked at the authentic Elvis Presley guitar, the authentic John Lennon songbook, the spark machine throwing electric light around the room, the street sign from Elvis Presley Boulevard. The place is the Smithsonian Institution of rock 'n' roll.

"We have these two guys on location in Miami," H. added. "They're twenty-six years old each. They charged the studio seventy thousand bucks for a pair of custom-made Porsche Carreras they had shipped from Germany right to the set. The guys took them home after one day's shooting and registered them in their own names. We told the producer and he said not to bother him because he was thinking. Fuck him. We'll charge them to his profit share and then we'll see how busy he is."

"It sounds as if you're having fun," I said.

"Oh, I'm having a great time," H. said. "I was down on the beach filming a scene with Don Johnson and there was this really pretty little extra. So Don says to her, 'Hey, darlin', how old are you?' And she says, 'Oooh, Mr. Johnson.' So he says, 'Darlin', how'd you like to have something to tell to *People* magazine?'"

"Wonderful."

"The next day, Don comes up to me and asks me if the little extra might possibly have a few speaking lines. Help her get her SAG card. You have to admire that in Don."

"What's that?"

"He keeps his promises."

We two men of the world nodded.

"Meanwhile everyone on the set is on a very short fuse, and whenever a take doesn't go right, Don yells at everybody, 'Hey, if you'd like to work on *The Equalizer*, just keep doing what you're doing.' And some people in my office are really acting like assholes."

"Like how?"

"Well, like in one episode that's coming up, Don meets this beautiful stewardess and takes her home and fucks her, and then she goes into convulsions and dies, and it turns out that she had a cocaine balloon in her stomach that burst, and Don has to track down the people who were using her as a mule."

"Sounds great to me."

"And one of the guys at Universal sent over a memo telling Michael Mann that the script didn't deal with Don Johnson's guilt. So Michael Mann says, 'What guilt?' and the guy at Universal says, 'Well, because they had sex and so Don Johnson must have jostled the cocaine balloon.'"

H. laughed. "The only good part was how happy it made Don Johnson when I told him about the memo. He agreed with it. 'It just shows that they know I have an eighteen-inch prick. Christ, I poked a hole in that goddamn balloon!'"

There we are, eating lunch at the Hard Rock Cafe listening to The Who, talking the inside dope on the hottest guy in TV, while my peers are filing motions, worrying about tuition at St. Alban's, and wondering how long until they can retire. Ain't life grand?

December 23, 1985

An unusual Monday lunch pitch to a woman TV producer who has an office on Melrose. The unusual part is that hardly anyone takes meetings the day before Christmas Eve. But this woman is a hard worker. Six months ago, she had a baby born three months premature. Both the mother and the baby were in intensive care, not expected to live, for two weeks. She recovered, and while she was still in intensive care at Cedars-Sinai, still hooked up to a blood-gas monitor, she was already taking pitches and reading scripts. Sounds right to me.

At this meeting, we had lunch at Le Duc. It is a small Vietnamese place right next to a store that sells leather bras and panties. Its name is SLUT. On the other side of Le Duc is a store that sells pajamas, trousers, blouses, sport jackets, all made up to look like war camouflage.

On the street in front of Le Duc, an angel-faced girl with fair skin, blue eyes, and black lipstick twirled a boa constrictor around her neck and watched glassily as the BMWs passed by.

The waiter told me that he had lost two daughters and his parents in the massacre by the NVA forces in Hue in 1968. I wish I could capture the look of stony, edgy contempt with which he watches the make-believe of the children on Melrose Boulevard. The lucky play games about pain and death. The rest of the world is in pain and dies.

"So here's my idea," I said to the woman. "There's this woman D.A. in New York. She's a fully alert, strong woman character, and she's called to the scene of a murder in a really fancy co-op on Madison Avenue. Two beautiful girls shot, and a janitor injured badly. And it's a really neat job, like a professional hit man or maybe even . . . a cop. . . ."

"I like it a lot so far," said the woman.

"And, to make a long story short, it turns out that a vice squad cop was 'on the pad' and was getting payoffs from the call girls. See, the girls who were shot were call girls, and the other call girls are afraid that none of the cops are honest, so they won't say a word, only the woman D.A. tracks down one ex-member of the call girl ring and it turns out that she's married to a famous Dallas surgeon, and she won't even think about revealing her past and going back to testify, and what d'ya know, she starts to crumble, and she goes back, and she even risks her life and her career and everything to testify. Pretty great, huh?"

"I like it a lot," the woman said. "You have a writer in mind?"

"Yeah," I said. "Me."

"You?" she asked in deep surprise. "I didn't know you wrote scripts."

"I do, and they're not bad. Try one."

"Maybe we should, just for this one, go with someone with network approval."

"I have network approval."

"Really?" the woman asked, looking doubtful.

"Well, I did one for a network not long ago."

"Did they make it?"

"No," I admitted grimly.

"Well, you might have lost your network approval."

"Let's call the network and see if I still have it."

"Okay, but in case you don't, let's think of alternative, network-approved writers. Just to be on the safe side."

"All right. Just to be on the safe side."

"Don't get me wrong. If you're network approved, it's all boss with me."

I walked out onto Melrose and walked alone toward a store that sells cookies. Who the hell could I call at the network to see if I still had network approval? I decided to call Lucinda DeMott. She's a member of the Inner Party as far as the networks go. She would know.

Lucinda and I had dinner chez Morton's. It was a quiet night. Many people have gone to The Ingleside Inn in Palm Springs. Others have gone to The Big Island to stay at The Mauna Kea. A few are in New York at The Sherry. And a few are in Hoboken with Mom.

We saw Steve Tisch and David Hoberman and a few other souls. We smiled and made flattering comments about people's weight. I asked Lucinda about getting to be network approved.

"The only qualification for any job in Hollywood is to get the job," Lucinda said to me. "Just remember that and you're all set."

"Okay."

A tough-looking woman agent came in. We smiled at her and told her how pretty she looked. She looked about as pretty as the boa constrictor I had seen this afternoon.

"God, I hate being friendly to all these people here," Lucinda said. "It makes me feel lonely."

"Why?"

"Because when I pretend I like these people, I feel as if that's someone else being nice, not me, and I don't even know who I am anymore, and that makes me feel lonely. I miss the real me, who would just as soon these people had never been born. I'm lonely for myself, if you know what I mean."

DECEMBER 24, 1985

Christmas Eve. I think I have to face the fact that something's wrong. It's the most festive, family-crazed time of the year and here I am sitting by the pool looking for pine needles that might have escaped the filter. Behind me, the dogs, Martha, Trixie, and Ginger, are all lined up in a neat row making sure I'm doing it right.

I went to lunch with Roy Ash at The Palm, but that just made me feel worse. Roy is a brilliant guy of about sixty-five. He started Litton Industries. He owns the largest gold mine in the world. He has a house with fifteen acres in Bel-Air, where even rich people have an eighth of an acre.

"You have unbelievable ideas, Ben," he said. "Incredible ideas."

We talked about buying a magazine, about why the stock market is not really efficient, about why most financial journalism is a fraud. At the end of the meal he shook my hand and told me what great ideas I have. Bear in mind, he makes far more in a day than I make in a whole year. Thus, his kind words bring to mind the perpetual crisis of my life: If I'm so smart, why aren't I rich? Why aren't I even close to rich? Why can't I even figure out a way to make a decent living?

After dinner at a Thai restaurant I drove down to see what was happening at the Hard Rock Cafe. It was closed. Pina Fini, next door, was almost closed.

Odo Riko, a new Japanese place, was open. I went into the bar and had my usual. A Diet Coke. The bartendress was a beautiful blond woman. The only other man in the bar was sobbing softly into his drink.

"This place is so dead," I said. "You're right here next to the busiest shopping center in America, the Beverly Center, but it's completely dead here."

The bartendress cupped her mouth and pointed at the sobbing Japanese man. "The owner," she whispered.

I nodded and started to leave. As I was walking out the door, the woman from the bar came up to me. "Listen," she said, "if you know of any other jobs . . ."

Just before I went to sleep, I started to read a book of memos written within Warner's before 1951. "A moving picture is just an expensive dream," Jack Warner said. "That's all it is, and hardly anybody knows it."

At three in the morning I was awakened by a sound. I went to the window. A man in a bathing suit was walking three dogs down the street. At three A.M.

At four A.M. another man across the street took out a garden hose and began to wash his car, all the while singing "Silent Night, Holy Night" in a soft, mournful rustle.

At five A.M. a long Cadillac limousine pulled up to the house where the man had just washed his car. The driver left the motor running, dashed into the house, then dashed out again. He looked carefully around, then got into the limo and drove away.

Silent Night. Holy Night.

DECEMBER 25, 1985

Merry Christmas. I slept until three in the afternoon. The only reason I woke up was that Traci and her sister Sonya appeared at the door to give me my Christmas present. Traci is the one who looks like Venus de Milo. Sonya looks like a young Sophia Loren. She is a student at the University of Arizona. She lives in a condo far outside of Tucson and spends much of her day watching soap operas.

"We love you, Ben," they both said. "Can we take Martha with us to our grandmother's nursing home?"

I told you I love children. They are such dearly mixed-up, exposed human beings, like layers of a mountain that has been exposed when a freeway is being blasted into it. You can see all their levels of greed and generosity and fear and exuberance. My puppies.

Dinner at the home of Michael and Michelle. They are Jewish, of course, but this is L.A., so they have a lavishly catered affair for their whole family, their in-laws, their sisters and cousins and aunts and nephews and nieces and long-lost friends, with little Christmas trees for everyone and small gifts of Irish linen.

At dinner, we played the usual Jewish dinner party game: "Can you top this idea for a novelty item even better than a Pet Rock, yet guaranteed to make a million dollars for you if the *momsers* don't steal it from you."

The entries:

- A plastic vest filled with water for summertime cooling wear
- A TV sitcom set in an old folks' home
- A child's toy in the shape of a lamb that turns into a motorcycle tough guy
- A dating game done transatlantic via satellite (my own entry)
- A root-beer-flavored toothpaste

The winner, by consensus, the water-filled vest for summer cooling.

We would all go out and manufacture that water-filled vest, see, except that once word got out about it, some big *bondit* like

Dow Chemical or Du Pont would steal the idea from us and take it all for themselves, the bastards.

DECEMBER 26, 1985

I dragged Rich Procter down to the Club Paradise at Figueroa and Olympic. It is next to a garbage-strewn parking lot. You have to walk up a flight of fiberboard stairs. Then you come to a fiberboard desk, where you pay your three dollars to get in. You walk along a threadbare carpet to a large room where six listless, plump, sallow women sit on green vinyl sofas. Across from them, separated by forty feet of Astroturf, is a cluster of Formica tables. Men sit at them, drinking orange juice, looking desperately at the women.

To the left of the men is a dance floor where about six couples were dancing in a dim light. A few of the girls on the dance floor looked like Filipinos. They danced slowly, languidly, as if they were selling nothing but time. In fact, that's exactly what they were doing. Thirty cents a minute, or about one-seventh what my shrink charged.

I approached a young woman who was slightly more alert-looking than the others. She was blond and discouraged. She had scars near her ears. She took a time clock to the fiberboard desk and had it punched. That meant my clock was running.

Her name was Liz. She was twenty-three. She came from the Valley. Reseda. She had tried the job because she thought it would be "a gas. . . ." Originally she had been working with her girlfriend, but her girlfriend didn't like the job. Liz made fifty dollars on a good night. If a man propositioned her, she would tell him she had to punch out. Sorry, but that's the way it is. She was saving up to pay for a drunk-driving ticket. "Only it wasn't my fault. I had two drinks, but my car had a flat tire, and that's why it was wobbling on the road. . . ." Ten minutes. Three dollars.

DECEMBER 31, 1985

Tora! Tora! Tora!

Alex is back from Arkansas. She had a great time inspecting her grandfather's grave in Prescott, and then she drove across the state line to visit her Big Mama and Big Daddy's graves in Idabel, Oklahoma. What fun! "I did it because who knows if I'll ever in my life get back to see them," she said as she went through her Christmas cards.

A New Year's Eve party at Spago. You have to be a friend of Wolfgang or of Bernard to even be allowed in. Plus, you have to pay eighty dollars per person. For that you get two slices of pizza, barely cooked, a strange foie gras in a kind of plum sauce, and then a delicious veal. You also get champagne and then a few Scotches. Also, you get to hear a steel band playing loud enough for a whole cruise ship, only they play in a space the size of your basement rec room.

Michael and Michelle were there. So was the captainess of industry and her husband. So was a man who had been a Hollywood actor, Ralph Lewis, and was now a mogul in the E. Gluck watch company.

Also at the dinner was a Bob Schwartz, who heads a maker of antimissile avionics named Loral. We spent most of the dinner talking about how an airplane might avoid an optical lock-on surface to air missile. Truth to tell, I don't know a thing about the subject, but here we were, at Spago, talking about visual signatures, photosensitive gallium arsenide, and chaff. It was swell.

I talked for a long time to Dabney Coleman. I talked for an instant to Alan Greisman, who was there with his glamorous wife, Sally Field, who kept smiling at me as if she knew me. I was about to talk to Lesley Ann Warren, but she looked worried, so I passed her up. Glenn Ford was sitting right behind me. Jon Avnet, the young millionette and producer, was there, necking with his wife. I admire that.

Alexander Godunov was there with what's-her-name . . . Jackie Bisset. They were both dressed like ragpickers on Melrose. They looked tired.

It was a swell evening, really a lot of fun. We got to sleep by two in the morning, and were ready for the New Year.

JANUARY 1, 1986

A journey on the 2:00 P.M. PSA flight from LAX to San Jose, en route to Santa Cruz. Almost all of the no-smoking section was taken up with little Hasidic children going back to San Jose from a trip to Disneyland. They yelled and screamed the whole time. I often wonder how Jewish children, who tend to be so undisciplined and untrained, become so disciplined in school and at work. What makes it happen? I also notice the same about Oriental children. They are famed for their discipline as adults and as Toyota assemblers. But as children, they are holy terrors. Maybe that's what it takes to make a child into a disciplined adult.

Santa Cruz is a town of about forty thousand on the northern edge of the Monterey Bay. It was a logging town, then a quarrying town, then it was nearly dead for decades. In the 1960s it revived as a hippie center and the site of the University of California. My opinion? It's the most beautiful place on earth.

From the UC campus, mostly grassy meadows and red-woods, you can see across Monterey Bay all the way to Carmel. At night the moonlight is so bright you can read *Siddhartha* standing in a meadow, far from any building. You can walk into a grove of redwoods so thick that at noon it is permanent cool evening.

On the main street, Pacific Mall, you see the sixties

preserved in amber, with panhandling hippies, women breast-feeding their infants, street musicians playing "Mr. Tambourine Man" with hats on the sidewalk in front of them, bars playing "The Gates of Eden" on their tape players, women at the next stool who ask you what your sign is, and what you'll do for them if they go back to your room at The Dream Inn.

Santa Cruz is also a world center of gingerbread, Victorian houses, surfing, and small religious cults who travel to the city in old school buses. It also has a small park set aside only for wandering hippies, so that in a tiny portion of Morgan Stanley America there is one plot that is forever Altamont.

As usual, I went for a walk around the UC campus. It was totally deserted. I saw no one as I walked along the piney paths and stared into empty classroom buildings. That gave me a slight tingle of fear, which gave me a more springy step than I might otherwise have had. After all, I can remember murders on that campus. Also near the campus. A lot of them. That was back in 1972 and 1973, when Santa Cruz was the murder capital of the nation on a per capita basis. There was the guy who shot a family for building a house and cutting down redwoods. There was another guy who murdered a family because he thought they cheated him when he bought a Smith & Wesson revolver from them. Then there was Ed K. the champ. He beheaded about eight young women in and around the campus. As it happened, he had some practice in psychosis. He had murdered his grandparents by burning down their house in 1960, and he had spent most of his life in state mental hospitals. When Ronald Reagan became governor, he decided the state did not need to spend money on all those old, stale mental cases. So Ed was released.

The problem was, he still had a grudge against his family. He was a little scared from all that time on shock corridor, so he killed fifteen-year-old girls instead for a while. But finally, when his mom asked him if he were the bad boy who was killing all those girls, he cut her head off, too, put her in the closet, then called the police and said he would like to go back to the mental hospital, please.

Anyway, Ed's been gone for twelve years, but I still worry about walking around alone on campus.

(I don't want to forget the "Trailside Killer," who waited along the paths in Cowell State Park, contiguous to the UC campus, for hikers he could kill. He was just convicted last year. He might be out by now, for all I know.)

I passed by the Japanese War Lord–style buildings of Porter College, then walked across a huge suspension footbridge over a deep ravine. A family of deer stared up at me from below the bridge. I walked across another bridge and then up a hill to a jumble of Aztec science buildings framed by a towering grove of redwood trees. In one of the auditoriums there, in 1972, I used to sit and watch film noir pictures—*Fallen Angel, Detour, Bad Girl*—with Mary, the puppy, my first dog, wrapped inside my jacket, fast asleep, a warm spot in the universe pressed against my chest.

Then down a hill and by the McHenry Library. It is a five-story, airy, glass and cement building like a hangar for spaceships bearing overdue library books, again, surrounded by redwoods, pines, and flowering bushes. When I first saw the library in 1972 I gasped out loud at its beauty, startling a hippie woman sleeping on the grass in front of it.

Then past the Baskin Art Center to a small courtyard facing over empty, grassy meadows leading down to the Pacific. The meadows are surrounded by small stands of redwood. Cattle graze there, languidly eating the tall grass, little knowing the particular form of use which their keepers have in mind for them.

I always have a good head of steam by the time I reach that clearing. My breath is coming fast and deep and regularly. My face is flushed and I feel strong and energetic, as if everything is possible.

Usually when I get to that overlook I have already thought of five new ideas for movies which I can try to sell. Today's best was about a blind date which starts out horribly but leads to the love of a lifetime. Sort of like *After Hours* but with a plot.

I also have a wonderful idea of how I can propose to General Electric that they restructure the company in a way which makes it even more the premier company of all time. Also, I usually have a number of ideas of various companies I can sue in class actions and make lots of money for us small stockholders.

In a word, I can stand in that little grass courtyard and look out at the world and still believe in the gospel as preached by movies: *That it will all turn out right in the end.*

I walk by the redwoods and the open fields and the solitary buildings with their lighted windows and their redwood guard houses, and look out at the ocean, and I know that no matter what has happened yesterday, tomorrow will be all right. Better than all right. Yesterday may have been broken hearts at ABC, dropping whole lines from my column in the *Herald-Examiner*, investment bankers humiliating me at the California Club, the brakes broken on the car for the fifth time in a month. Yesterday may have been a quick, hurtful step toward dust.

But tomorrow Michael Eisner will call from Disney and tell me they cannot live without me, Michael Milken will call from Drexel and tell me they will fail without my insight, Dr. Surrey will call and tell me they made a mistake on the tests and we will have a perfect boy and girl riding tricycles around the house in a few days. Tomorrow will be a golden, sunlit jog past soft, cuddly deer to eternal life.

I keep telling you, that's what the movies have taught me. That's what the movies have taught every American. They have imprinted in our minds America's unique secular religion, the established church of American life, the Cinematic Faith—that it will all turn out right in the end.

Despite all the evidence of reality, despite the fact that Dachau was already running full steam when *Gone with the Wind* was made, still the faith of the movies is my guide. Yea, though I walk through the valley of the shadow of Death, about halfway through the third act John Wayne will rescue me and Debra Winger will confess that she loves me and Edward Arnold will make me a partner in his bank. This is not foolishness. This is my birthright as an American.

I inherit it when I stand at the top of a hill in Santa Cruz and look across to the Bay of Monterey.

I also inherit it when I sit in a darkened theater and watch a good movie.

After the Inspirational Walk, I went back to my room at The Dream Inn to rest. At eight my pal Angela appeared. "Angie" is twenty years old. She comes from Portugal. She wants to be a model. Her roommate used to work for me, so I agreed to talk to her.

Angie was pretty, with high cheekbones, a ski slope nose, light blue eyes, and light pink lips. She had a portfolio of photos, including photos in lingerie, and I daresay she looked great. Alluringly mean and sexy.

We went to dinner at a Chinese restaurant next to the wharf. The night was drizzly, cold, and foggy. We were the only people in the restaurant except for an ancient Chinese cook who remembered me from other visits and wrung his hands in joy. Across from us, a huge gray miasma rolled back and forth onto the sand like an outrageously overgrown beach ball. Scary-looking punks with leather jackets walked back and forth by the window, smoking reefers, snapping their fingers, shaved heads hunched forward against the cold.

Across the street was the Coconut Grove. It is a boardwalk dance hall and pinball parlor about the size of Madison Square Garden. It has curlicues and arches and looks as if it were made from concrete poured around a mold of a Busby Berkeley stage set, and maybe it was. Tonight it was closed and dark except for a pink and gray sign flashing on and off in the fog saying COCONUT GROVE.

Angie had an entire bottle of Bonny Doon Riesling. She told

me about her adventures in drinking contests at bars, driving on acid over mountain passes, swimming naked with hubby in high surf.

"Good night, Angie," I said. "Don't call us. We'll call you."

Still, the evening had atmosphere. By and large I will take the atmosphere and the fantasy over the fact, and Angie is proof of how right I am.

January 2, 1986

On my way back from Burbank airport, I passed by the gleaming, mirrored Warner Brothers building across from the Burbank Studios. Not too far away is the Burger Ballroom, which also serves Mexican food. I felt like eating an enchirito made with beans, so I pulled in. As I stood in line behind the messengers and the welfare mothers, I spied a cunning, little face behind the counter.

"Hi, Marcie," I said. "I'd like an all beef enchirito. No, make that an all-bean enchirito."

Marcie looked up at me slyly through her eyelashes. "Hi, Ben," she said without missing a beat. "Anything to drink?"

"Medium Diet Pepsi."

She wrote it down, then passed on the message to her colleagues at the Burger Ballroom assembly line.

"Listen," she whispered conspiratorially, "can you get me out of here?"

"Are you being held against your will?" I asked.

"What's that mean?"

"Nothing. How did you get this job if you're only fourteen?"

"Well, I just turned fifteen and it's part of the work experience program at my high school, and I have to work here for three hours a day, and all I get paid is minimum wage."

"That's not so bad. At least you get good food."

"Yes, but I should be earning a lot more than that. I want a car like yours. Soon."

"Well, I don't know how you're going to do that," I said.

"Think about it," she said, looking me straight in the eye. "Think about it. How would I get that kind of money at my age?"

I thought about it while I sucked on my Diet Pepsi.

"I thought nobody could touch you until you were sixteen or something. No matter how much they wanted to."

"I didn't mean that *no one* could, you know," she whispered. "I meant no one could do it for free and not take care of me, you know."

"Oooh, I see."

"You must make a lot of money, driving around in that car."

"Not really," I said. "Driving around in that car costs me money. A lot of it. You'd be surprised."

Marcie smiled and turned sideways and stretched upward as if she were reaching for a volleyball on a beach. She smiled at me as she did. She looked older than fifteen. She also looked very healthy.

"Just think about it," Marcie said. "I thought you did a great job in that movie, by the way."

"Thanks," I said. "You're a pal."

JANUARY 3, 1986

Dinner with my pal H., the executive at Universal who works on *Miami Vice*. We ate at Le Duc, my new favorite place.

We had cashew chicken, and shrimp coated with coconut, and H. said, "So we're having Bush on the show, playing himself, going along with the Drug Enforcement Agency while they're running around South Florida chasing drug dealers in speedboats."

"How did that happen?"

"He called up, or one of his guys called Michael Mann, and Michael says, 'Hey, Bush wants to be on the show. Is that okay?' So on the corporate side, we all said it was okay, so now it's happening."

"Ain't life grand."

"You know, the shows this year on *Miami Vice* haven't really been that good. You have any ideas about how they could be better?"

"Absolutely," I said. "Try having the beginning, middle, and end of the shows have something to do with each other. Try having Crockett and Tubbs be the same when the show is half over as when it begins. Try having Crockett and Tubbs stop acting as if they were caricatures of themselves and start acting like actors, or like people trying to act. Stop having it be a cardboard cut-out imitation of two pimps out on the town looking for a good time. Try having Crockett and Tubbs act as if they had feelings instead of sneering at everything that happens in Miami. That might work."

"In other words, you want Don Johnson to stop acting like himself, and you want some doctor to give Philip Michael Thomas a brain."

JANUARY 4, 1986

Have I told you how much I hate my car? Have I told you how I'm fighting a perpetual battle with it, how it simply waits to torture me and make my life miserable on every occasion?

Latest example: its stupid fucking little computer brain has the idea that the brakes aren't working. I've had the brakes fixed ten times in the last two years and the mechanics at Merlin Olsen Porsche say they're perfect. Never mind. Every time I touch the brake pedal, two, not one, but two giant lights flash on the dashboard vivid and red, with exclamation points in them.

I feel as if I am driving a creature that is out of control, hateful, eager to hurt me. It is not carrying me around town. It's beating on me, trying to make me suffer.

Every day I plot to get rid of it. But selling a Porsche 928 is impossible. Why? No one in his right mind wants one. They cost a fortune, never work, take about five thousand of maintenance a year to make them run, and don't go any faster than a Honda CRX.

The monster uses almost ten dollars' worth of gasoline to go to Beverly Hills and back, a distance of about twenty miles, maybe less. Sometimes it refuses to start. Sometimes it makes loud clicking noises on the freeway at seventy miles per hour. When I pull it up to the Merlin Olsen repair shop, the mechanics—who get a percentage of the bill—actually start to giggle like children about to get a present from a rich uncle.

A slight irregularity in the engine idle?

"No problem, Herr Shtein. Six hundred dollars."

A smashed window from thieves stealing my radio one of the four times they have done it this last twelve months?

"What a shame, Professor Doktor. Nine hundred dollars not counting the radio."

So you see. The goddamned car is a vampire, sucking out my blood and making me weak.

Long ago, when I first moved here, I had to have a Mercedes. It was proof that I believed in my own future. Then another Mercedes. Then this Porsche. I spend more on repairing these cars and insuring them than I spend on our mortgage.

"You must be rich to have a car like that." Marcie says it. Trish says it. Mexicans and Syrians at the gas station say it.

"No. I would be rich if I didn't have it." I say that.

The cunning evil of the car is that not only can I not sell it because no one will buy it, but it is so goddamned good-looking it would make you sob. It is long and low and sleek and powerful. Its *weinrote metallike* finish gleams even in the dark. It can sometimes go eighty up a steep hill without a murmur.

When I stop at a light, male drivers in 450 SLs whistle at my car. Young women in Toyotas smile appraisingly. ("Not me, girls, I'm not the one you want. I'm a writer, you little fools.")

Today, I steeled myself to buy a Toyota myself. Why not? They never break. Never. They never have lights that say "Warning, you are about to die!" on a flashing red background. They're cheap, solid, and dependable.

The problem was that as I started to drive out onto Mulholland to head toward North Hollywood Toyota, I passed two beautiful girls in miniskirts taking pictures of the city spread below. They turned around and looked at my car. The blond one, the one who looked like Morgan Fairchild at twenty, shouted, "Rad car, mister!"

I pulled over and smiled at the two girls. One of them ran over to the car, then the other one. "Great car, mister," they said. "You live near here?"

So there's the problem. There is no Toyota ever made which would get two teenage girls in miniskirts to run over and flirt with a brainoed-out forty-one-year-old.

When I first moved here, I used to stare at the men in gleaming black 450 SLs and wish I could be like them. Now I know what being one of them is: penitential, painful visits to the repair shop, using a smelly rental car while your car waits for a part that has to be shipped in from Ulm, in the Eastern Zone, knowing that you could have a secure retirement if you did not have that car, enslavement to a false fantasy image of yourself.

Now I envy the nerds in their Toyotas. They will not have to go on welfare when they are sixty-five. They will eat caviar while my wife and I eat dog food. The nerds in their Toyotas do not have a vampire sucking on their balls, disguised as a car.

But then, tonight, when we took Michael and Michelle to Morton's for their anniversary, the thin blond, Lisa, who works in front of the restaurant, looked out at the demon car and smiled. "What a gorgeous car you have," she said. "I think it's the best-looking car we ever get here at Morton's."

So you see the problem. The Toyota and good sense will just have to wait.

JANUARY 9, 1986

Remember when I told you about *Krypto*? About my shrink telling me it was not going to get made, then someone at the studio telling me that it would get made?

Well, *Krypto* was just a code word. And really it's a miniseries, not a movie. It's about a family in America ten years after the Soviet occupation. I brought the idea for it to a network executive two and a half years ago, and the network executive ran with it. I wanted it to be a short, possibly satiric, homily about freedom and consumerism, but the network didn't care what I wanted. They had their own grand ideas. I fought with them and got a lowly position as an informal consultant, which means nothing. But I got money, enough to buy a new Porsche, a single card in the main titles, and the novelization rights. I did not write the script, or get any screenplay rights at all.

But in the last few days there has been some amazing excitement around the project, which is tentatively titled *Amerika*.

Last Friday, in Moscow, a group of Russian "artists," official pals of the KGB, including Yevgeny Yevtushenko and Igor Moiseyev, appeared at the Foreign Ministry and told the United States that they did not like *Rambo* and *Rocky IV* and *Red Dawn*. Yevtushenko said they were cruel to the peace-loving Russian people.

Most of all, said the Russkies, they did not want a certain miniseries called *Amerika* to air on Amerikanski televisionski next fallski.

In fact, the KGB is so upset about the miniseries that they called in the head of the ABC News Bureau in Moscow and told him they would have to reconsider even having an ABC bureau in Moscow if ABC did not cancel the show.

Now, when I was just days away from having a project "of mine" begin principal photography, for the first time ever, it was put on ice, not by a stupid production executive or a star who wouldn't sign his contract. No, for the first time in the history of Hollywood, a project was stopped at least temporarily by the weight and cunning of the KGB. And it was my project. I calls that fate.

JANUARY 13, 1986

Ups and downs.

At breakfast, I got a call from T., a major studio head to whom I had sent my favorite script, *My Grownup*.

"I loved the hell out of that thing," he said. "I can't tell you how much I loved it."

"Thank you."

"You have a better style, really and truly, than Bob Towne or Bill Goldman. I don't know why you haven't really been put on the map yet."

"I don't either."

"I think you can count on us to move that script forward, and especially to try to find a really fantastic location that fits the story perfectly, like maybe Elstree could make us something in England."

"The story is set in Santa Cruz," I said. "Why would we want to have a set made in London?"

There was a long pause on the line. "What about the part in the atomic submarine after the high school kids have taken it over and are threatening to blow up New York?"

"Honestly, I don't know what you're talking about," I said. "My script is about 'The Graduate' twenty years down the road. About him falling for a young girl and then falling head over heels for her mother."

There was a long silence once again on the line. "Who is this?" T. asked.

"Ben Stein," I said. "My agents sent over *Grown-Up*."

"You mean that thing about the congressman having the affair with the college girl? That was sick. That was really a sick idea. Who would ever want to go with something like that?"

"Well, it worked out pretty well for Stanley Kubrick," I said.

"In what? In *2001*? I don't remember any of that older man–younger woman stuff."

"No, in *Lolita*."

"What's that?"

"It's a movie. It made a lot of money. About Humbert H. Humbert and Lolita. His little girlfriend."

"Who?" T. asked sharply.

"Humbert Humbert and Lolita," I said.

"Who are they?" T. asked. "People in some book, or what?"

JANUARY 18, 1986

Dinner with Marty K., an executive at Disney, at Matoi, a fabulously good Japanese restaurant.

"Remember how you told me the only qualification for getting anything in Hollywood was to get it?"

"I remember," I said.

"One corollary: the only disqualification for getting anything in Hollywood is wanting it badly."

A Messiah come to judgment. At the sushi bar.

January 20, 1986

A meeting at the Burbank Studios to discuss one of my projects. The general idea is a TV movie, an exposé of the for-profit hospital centers that supposedly treat alcoholism and other forms of addiction, but are just rip-offs. The studio has gotten a wonderful TV star, Linda Lavin, involved in the project. She has enormous TV juice, because she played "Alice" for many years on CBS. We have a major writer, S., a middle-aged woman with a sad, sensitive face, a representative of the studio, Norman Stephens, a Princeton man with a cable-knit sweater to prove it, and a powerful agent, Marty L., to make the right moves at the network.

We sat and talked about how the movie might go. "There are all kinds of addictions," S. said. "There are addictions to shopping and to money. Then there are addictions to the wrong people. You can actually be addicted to a lover who is bad for you, like drugs, but something about him makes you addicted to him. That happens and it's just as hard to get off the lover as it is to get off cocaine. You get addicted to the very fact that he's so wrong for you."

"Can we dramatize that?" Linda Lavin asked. "I think that's an aspect of addiction that no one has touched yet."

"I think so," S. said.

"I wonder if we can also touch on how people refuse to get in touch with their feelings when they're addicted, and when they stop being addicted, they get in touch with their feelings, and that's what hurts." I said that. I said it as I looked out the window onto Barham Boulevard and saw a man my age walk by holding a small girl child with blond hair on his shoulders while she squealed and pointed at the silver windows in the Warner Brothers building.

S., who saw what I was looking at, and also saw me, touched my arm and said, "We can dramatize it."

We all talked for another hour. It would be easy for me to pretend that the meeting was all Hollywood jargon and false praise and buzzwords. It would be easy, but it would be wrong. In fact, the men and women in Linda Lavin's office were really and truly trying to do something wonderful. With the best will in the world, they were trying—we were trying—to make a drama that will tell Americans how to stop wrecking their lives, and how to vibrate to the beauty of a sunset off Zuma Beach.

Only rarely do I get to be in meetings with so many people saying such sensitive words, trying so hard to be good. But each meeting is a jewel, and a powerful proof that I am right to be in Hollywood. Nowhere else do smart people sit around and try to figure out how they can tell the truth, make strangers whole, and make art. Of course, we are all also trying to make a living. But to make a living helping human beings to stop torturing themselves is a particularly good way to make ends meet.

After the meeting, I went to the Burger Ballroom and ate an enchirito. Marcie smiled slyly at me as she threw bean paste onto a tortilla shell. The sun reflected off the Warner Brothers building. A row of royal palms marched by in reflection, three floors up. Another man with a little daughter sat next to me and ate tacos. The little girl dripped taco sauce onto her jacket and laughed. These are the good old days.

JANUARY 22, 1986

S. and I have been assigned to do further research into rip-off addiction treatment centers. I called up a place called the "Compassion Center" in Glendale, and S. and I went out to talk to them. On the way, we stopped for Japanese food at Teru Sushi.

S. asked me about my life. I told her the basics—law school, marriage, divorce, remarriage. S. looked at me sadly. "I'm just getting a divorce," she said. "I would love to be able to hope that someday my husband and I would get back together."

"I think you can," I said. "You both have to realize that you love each other. Then you have to realize that he's the best man in the world for you, and you're the best woman in the world for him. When you realize that, then you have to start taking care of each other, and making your little family the center of your lives, instead of a place to hang your hat between deals."

"That's a lot to do," S. said. "I was head of the motion picture division at CMA, which was the forerunner of ICM, before I was forty. My husband has the most Academy Awards for composing of anyone in history. I never really heard of a story like yours. It's a different way to live."

Even though S. is a former agent, I cannot help but love her. If she can write as well as she shows her feelings, we will have a major TV movie here.

As we chewed our tempura, jazz music came over the stereo at Teru Sushi. S. looked even more delicately touched. "This is an album my husband produced. He plays keyboards on it as well," she said. "You can tell his touch. It's very sharp and distinct, yet soft. You can hear the way his touch is over the stereo." She looked down at her plate and tears came to her eyes. "I have a meeting with my lawyer about this tomorrow," she said. "I'd like to bring this music along, so my lawyer could know how I feel about his touch at the keyboards, his touch . . . I don't know. A lawyer would never understand."

"No," I said. "He wouldn't understand. But you understand, and that's what counts."

"It used to count," she said.

I have hardly ever worked with anyone with the sensitivity of S., the agent, writer, and divorcee. God, I hope she writes as beautifully as she sounds.

The Compassion Center is on the third floor of the most boxy, nondescript medical building imaginable. Both S. and I pretended to need treatment. We said we were brother and sister. We were ushered out of the elevator and into a gray waiting area: gray linoleum floors, gray vinyl walls, gray nurses' station, gray signs on the walls. The nurses laughed and screamed about something on *The Young and the Restless*. I read the offering brochure of the hospital. After a few minutes I got up and walked down the hall to the patients' "play room." It reminded me of the activities room at the home for old people where I take the dogs on Sundays. It had the same used games, the same used books, the same hopeless grime on the folding tables.

A man with a beard and a synthetic smile put his arm on my shoulder. "Are you the brother from the brother and sister team?" he asked. His voice was a deep, rich, phony bass. "I'm Scott. I'm the director of the program," he said. "I hope we can help you."

"I hope so," I said.

We walked down the hall to see Leon, the "intake counselor." Scott, the program director, assured me that he could already see both my addiction and my wish to be cured. "I can see it in your eyes," he said. "All the booze and pills and pot, and the hope that you can get your life in order."

"I'm so glad," I said. "I'm so glad someone finally sees."

In fact, of course, I almost never drink, never smoke anything, and am addicted only to the soft, furry faces of my dogs, Martha, Trixie, and Ginger.

Leon was a hugely fat man in his fifties. "I can see where it hurts," he said. "Have you got insurance?"

"Yes, I do," I said. "How much does it cost to be here?"

"Basically, it runs ten thousand for four weeks," he said. "But your insurance will probably cover it, so there's really not much that'll come out of your pocket."

"What do we do here?"

"We have breakfast, and then meditation, and then group therapy, and then clean-up detail, and then lunch, and then field trips to the zoo, and then more group therapy."

"Wonderful," I said. "Do I get to see a psychiatrist?"

"Well, you can see a psychiatrist if you want, and we have our very own psychologist on staff, and you can see him as often as you want."

"For the ten thousand?"

"No, every time you see him, that's an extra hundred dollars, but your insurance will probably pay for it."

"Who leads the group therapy?"

"One of the patients, or else a counselor, who usually has credentials for a six-month program in alcoholism counseling from the local junior college," Leon said. "Very well trained."

"So you mean I'm going to be treated by a person with a certificate from a junior college?"

"Exactly," Leon said cheerfully.

"So I'm paying three hundred dollars a day, and I don't get to see a shrink at all?"

"You can see one anytime, but you have to pay extra," Leon said.

"So what does the money go for?"

"Well, it goes for the group therapy and the field trips and the room," he said.

Leon lit his third Parliament. "I can tell you're an intelligent gentleman," he said. "You'll like it here."

"Look, Leon," I said. "I'm really in desperate pain when I don't get the Percodan I've been taking."

"How many do you take every day?"

"Oh, at least six," I said. I have no idea how many Percodan an addict takes, but it was apparently a good guess.

"A real junkie," Leon said happily. "We don't want you to suffer. If it's too hard on you, we can give you something to wean you off the Percodan gradually."

"What would that be?"

"Valium," he said, wetting his lips. "IV. As much as you need."

I could have sworn he winked.

"So I'll get off drugs, but if it's too hard, I'll be able to get some Valium, right?"

"Right," Leon said. "Can I get down the name of your insurance plan and a few numbers here to make sure you're covered?"

While Leon noted the numbers from my Blue Cross card, he inhaled so deeply that in one puff he turned half of his cigarette to ash. "I can tell you're a real gentleman," he said. "I used to spend a lot of time with real gentlemen. A lot of time on Wall Street, with brokers and speculators. You might say I'm in the same line they are."

"What's that?" I asked.

"Brokers. Only I'm selling a new life. A new way to start living and start saving your own life."

"Brokers get a commission on each sale."

"I know," Leon said, looking into my eyes and smiling. "I have to make a living, too, same as everybody else."

S. and I drove back along Ventura Boulevard. We passed every kind of shop and stall imaginable. The Rice Bowl. The Tacos el Carbon. The Huevos Conquistadores. The Burger Pit. Gold and Silver Bought and Sold. Discount Tires. Toyotas. Subarus. Porsches and BMWs.

The marketplace that is Los Angeles. If you think of Los Angeles as one immense market, like the casbah in Tehran, you get a good purchase on the place.

Everyone is selling all the time. Don't expect grassy court-yards like there are in Cambridge, because there are no grassy courtyards in bazaars. Don't expect beautiful public buildings like the Capitol or the White House in the casbah. Every inch must be used for stall space. To sell. If you expect Los Angeles to be a huge outdoor market, a casbah and flea market that never stops, you are not disappointed. You do not feel like killing a man who sells spaces in the Compassion Center for ten thousand a month on commission. If you think of Los Angeles as one huge trading pit, it's not crazy that a Compassion Center does not offer trained psychologists except as a high dollar option, but does offer Valium, IV. After all, Valium is a lot cheaper than a psychologist's time. In the bazaar, time is money, and no one really expects anyone else to care whether anyone else lives or dies.

There is one law in the trading pit: make the sale, and all the Compassion Center and smiles and nurses' stations and group therapy are only tools for the trained closer to get the signature on the check.

JANUARY 23, 1986

A gift in the mail from my smart friend Victoria in Washington, D.C. It was a Japanese version of *Elvis' Greatest Hits,* with a full color portrait of the young Elvis Presley stamped onto the vinyl. Those Japanese. The first song on the album was "Ready, Teddy."

Playing it—like playing any of my oldies favorites—was like staring into the Proustian tealeaves. "Ready, Teddy" was one of my faves, and was also the fave of my boyhood next-door neighbor, Carl Bernstein.

Carl used to sit in his study and play "Ready, Teddy" on the guitar. We were about twelve years old. Carl, ever creative, had made up his own words to the song, mocking his eighth-grade shop teacher.

> Russell, Troxel,
> Go, man, go,
> I've got a witch that
> I love so . . .

It was pretty good. It rhymed and fit the beat. As far as I was concerned in 1957, it would probably be Carl's greatest accomplishment.

After all, Carl never studied, had a messy room, wore his shirttail out, had long hair, and smoked like a maniac. A *shondah* for all of us nice Jewish boys on Harvey Road in Silver Spring, Maryland. Carl once told his eighth-grade homeroom teacher that the room smelled like a Chinese whorehouse because someone had spilled her perfume. He was suspended from school for three days, a disgrace for the whole street, and I had to walk home with him along Dale Drive to break it to his mother. She did not like the news, bawled him out, and I left.

So Carl made up an imitation of "Ready, Teddy," and he never got any credit for it. On the other hand, he did get a lot of mileage out of Richard Nixon and John Mitchell, and Nora Ephron got a lot of mileage out of him. You see how life goes. I often read about Carl and Nora, or Carl and Gloria Emerson, or Carl and Elizabeth Taylor, or Carl at Elaine's. Pretty soon now, I'll get to see Carl in *Heartburn* from my wife's studio, Paramount. But only Carl and I remember his imitation of "Ready, Teddy." It was damned good.

JANUARY 25, 1986

Lunch with Traci at the Hard Rock Cafe. The food is cheap and delicious. Traci had a salad and I had ice cream. "I don't know about this new guy I met at a party. He's always antsy about the police, and he has this mail order business that's kind of a scam."

"It sounds like he's a total confidence man," I said.

"He is not!" Traci said indignantly. "He's a drug dealer!"

January 27, 1986

Tonight was the world premiere of the new John Hughes movie, *Pretty in Pink*. It was a lush affair. At the Mann's Chinese Theater and everything. We parked our car next to the beat-up, richly tail-finned Cadillac convertible of Alex Godunov and his close personal friend, Jackie Bisset. As always, they looked tired. There were fans screaming for their autographs. The Brat Pack was every-where. Andrew McCarthy, Molly Ringwald, Jonathan Cryer. John Hughes was there with his steel-rimmed Trotsky glasses. Michael Chinich was there, dressed in black, as always. Marian Chinich looked hip and gorgeous, as always.

The movie was cute. It isn't designed for forty-one-year-olds, but I liked it anyway. It was about a poor girl who gets dumped on by a rich guy and then gets him back. In high school. In Van Nuys. Or Baltimore. Or maybe in Chicago. Somewhere out there in America where teenagers still get upset about going to the prom with the right guy. It was really touching when Molly Ringwald walked off with Mr. Right, looking all sweet and virginal in her pink dress from J.C. Penney. It'll probably make as much money for John Hughes as the whole J.C. Penney corporation made last year.

Afterward, there was a big party at The Palace. We all milled around and watched Cher and Josh Donen, Michael Fox and a tough-looking girl, and Molly Ringwald as they all talked to photographers and cameramen.

Alex went to talk to a lawyer about copyrights. I felt a tug at my sleeve. Yep.

"Hi, Marcie," I said. "How do you get invited to all these parties?"

"I just know the right people," she said with a smile. She wore what looked like a huge pajama top and horizontally striped socks. Like a combination of Baby Doll and Alice in Wonderland.

"Will you get me a drink?" she asked. "I'm not old enough, and the bartenders won't serve me."

"Oh, I bet they will if you smile at them."

"Yeah, I bet they will," she said.

"You like to drink?"

"Not as much as I like to base," she said with an eager smile.

"Excuse me?"

"Free base, man. I love it so much. I like to just sit around for hours with my friends. We argue about who gets the next hit. It's so weird. I love it."

"That's great," I said. "What a wonderful way to live."

"Yeah," she said. "When I was really young, like just a little kid, I mostly did angel dust. Every day after school, I'd have a Kool dipped in dust. I'd get so fried, it was fantastic. Then I started doing acid. At school. It was so great going to school on acid. Really great. I'd be tripping and I didn't even know where I was."

"Gosh, it sounds great. Can I try some?"

"Really?" she squealed. "You really want some?"

"No, not really."

This is perfect. In John Hughes's movies, the kids are all virgins and the biggest thing they worry about is who gets to take Molly Ringwald to the prom, which is cool. In Hollywood, the fourteen-year-olds are basing like crazy and fighting over who gets the next hit and who brought the rubbing alcohol. I want to go home and live in a John Hughes movie.

Which I may soon be able to do! John told me I was in the editor's cut of *Ferris Bueller's Day Off*, for two long scenes, and that spells F-A-M-E to me. God, get me out of my office and in front of the cameras! And as far as possible from real life.

MARCH 7, 1986

Let me tell you where I have been.

Since our last communication, I have been on a trip to Florida with my goddess wife. We visited Disney World. We rode the monorail blue, gold, and purple. We saw the twelve-screen movie about Canada. It was the most exciting movie experience I have ever had, and it is only twenty minutes long. We saw the robots who play Jefferson and Franklin at the American pavilion at EPCOT. Perhaps Michael Eisner might want to rethink that one. Robots playing the Founding Fathers is not quite a joke and not quite serious. We walked through an aviary and saw flocks of flamingos, two perfect bald eagles with defiant eyes inside cages. We rode on a launch across a cool, crisp lake all by ourselves with sharp spray hitting us in the face and our hands in each other's pockets.

After Disney World, we drove up to Gainesville. I had been solicited to be a visiting professor at the University of Florida. It was an exercise in self-deception. The professors looked at me suspiciously. What would I, a Jew from Hollywood, possibly want in their department of "journalism and public relations"? One of them asked me if I had ever written any magazine articles. "About five hundred," I said.

"Yes, but have you ever taught?"

"At American University, at Harvard, and at UC, Santa Cruz," I answered.

"Yes, but have you ever taught in the South?" he asked.

So, you see. I had an idea that teaching in a small town might be a distraction. That was self-deception. When you have lived and played in the Hollywood playpen, you cannot just go off to any other schoolyard.

The high point of my trip—just so you know what kind of guy I am—was our farewell dinner at a fake pirate ship restaurant in downtown Gainesville, an adorable restored, gentrified small town center. I went to the telephone to call Traci, my Valley Girl, and get my phone messages from her.

For ten rings, there was no answer. Then Traci breathlessly came on the line. "Where are my messages?" I asked.

"I forgot to get them," Traci said. "Well," she added hastily, "I didn't really forget. What happened was that I was at your house, and Ginger jumped over the fence and started to chase a car. So I ran after her, and she started to run after a limousine on Mulholland. So I caught her, and brought her home. Then I noticed the limousine in front of your house. I thought the guys in it looked like Arabs, so I thought maybe they were assassins from Libya. So I got in your car and drove away, sort of winking at them, and they followed me. And I drove all over downtown L.A. and I finally lost them, and by the time I lost them, it was rush hour, and I didn't want to go across town in that traffic."

"I understand," I said. "Can you get my messages now?"

"Yes," she said. "Yes, I can."

A half-hour later, I called again. Traci was at our house. "You have about ten messages from people who want to buy the rights to one of your articles," she said. "What should I do about it?"

"Movie or TV rights?"

"I don't know," Traci said. "ABC called, so I guess that's uh, uh . . ."

"Okay. Call back everyone and say I'd love to make a deal, but I have to write the script. Okay?"

Now, get this. As I was having this jazzy, glamorous conversation, a woman of about twenty-five in tight light blue jeans and a yellow sweater and light blue eyes appeared at the pay phone in the fake pirate ship. She looked at me, at the cigarette machine next to me, then carefully, deliberately bent over at the waist supposedly to examine the choice of cigarettes. As she did, she poked her ass into my waist, then into my hip, and pressed against me, and giggled.

Then she stood up, just as I got off the phone. "Wow," she said. "That was great. You doing a play at the university?"

"No," I said. "I'm from Hollywood. I was talking about whether an article of mine should be a movie or a TV show."

"Wow," she said. "How long you here?"

"I'm leaving tomorrow," I said.

"Well, if you're ever back in G-burg, come over and see me. I work the bar here."

Then she opened the door into the dining room, gave me a meaningful bump, and walked back to the bar.

I liked that. We old married guys with paunches and three dogs don't get too much flirting. We treasure what we get.

In fact, given the choice of interest from a studio in an article or interest from a girl in me, I will take the girl anytime. That makes me gay by Hollywood standards, but that's the way I am.

Anyway, so that's where I've been. Plus, I have come down again with the L.A. flu, which is that flu you never get rid of. Never. When there's a relapse, it's a relapse into being well, and it never lasts.

MARCH 8, 1986

Ah, but then there is Richard Nixon.

Last night Roy and Lila Ash gave a lavish dinner party for the president. He had come to town to speak to the World Affairs Council, and now he was here in the room with us at the Regency Club in Westwood. He stood in the receiving line with Roy and Lila. As always, he looked like a Nixon mask of himself, with his jowls, his nose, his bushy eyebrows.

Roy introduced me to him, but he was all set for me before

that. "Our intellectual," he said. "I loved your piece in the *Times* about how Republicans have to have compassion. I loved that. And it's completely true."

"Thank you, Mr. President," I said. "How is Mrs. Nixon?"

"You'd never know she'd had a stroke," he said. "Great personality.

"Still writing?" he asked.

"Oh, absolutely," I said. "Every day."

He looked at Alex. "How does it feel to be married to a genius?" he asked her with a wink.

"It feels swell," Alex said, also with a wink.

At dinner, we sat with a table of wealthy Angelenos who completely ignored us. After dinner, R.N. answered questions. I asked one about whether the United States would survive for another hundred years. To give R.N. credit, and it is richly due, he took my question and gave a little rundown about me and my writing and he then said some nice things about my mother and father.

By this point, the wealthy people at our table were starting to look at Alex and me much more carefully.

"Will we survive another hundred years? I know we should. We have the economic power. America and Japan and Western Europe dwarf the Communist countries. We have the imagination. We have the brains. What we lack is willpower. Especially in the key centers of the nation. The willpower to go the distance. I worry about that, too.

"But I think in the final analysis, we will win, and I have to believe that we will win because we are right. I just have to believe that right will win."

Then he smiled at me and took another question.

In a few minutes, the crowd broke up. I walked out with Alex. Nixon stood by the elevator and then went down. Even in that crowd of people who had loved him since he was a congressman, he looked thoughtful, almost lonely. To me, R.N. has always been a sensitive poet locked up in a politician's body. He's not a robot like those displays at Disney World. He's a person. He's got a real spirit living inside him. He's a demon to people in Hollywood. He's a friend to me.

MARCH 15, 1986

Oooh, I have some very juicy gossip. Very, very juicy. Very hot stuff.

Remember how about eight years ago, Roman Polanski was charged with having sex with a thirteen-year-old girl while he was over at Jack Nicholson's house? Then Roman Polanski fled the country. Remember?

Well, this evening, while I was watching Ronald Reagan give his speech about aiding the Contras in Nicaragua, I got a call from my friend M. at a studio.

"I just spent the afternoon with the girl who fucked Roman Polanski and made him leave the country," he said.

"Who is she?"

"It's ———," he said. He named a girl, now a young woman, who happens to be a major sitcom star on a long-running show, now in national syndication.

I quickly computed if ——— were the right age—namely, thirteen in 1978. She was!

Plus, I had heard that the child-star had been a wild item, and that her mother had been a righteous, overbearing maniac, like most stage moms. It sounded perfect, but I don't know what to do about it. There is no action consequence, so to speak, except to feel as if I am on the inside. I guess that's worth something.

I hung up the phone and went back to watching President Reagan talk about the Contras and the Sandinistas.

MARCH 17, 1986

Remember that TV movie I told you about? The one about the rip-off alcoholism treatment centers? The one where everyone was so in touch with their feelings and loved the project so much? The one with Linda Lavin, who starred in *Alice* for ten years and has so much juice at the network that no one could even imagine her getting turned down for a project she really cared about? The one where the network executive said she thought this was going to be an Emmy winner for sure?

The network turned it down. It's too much like another TV movie they did a few years ago about high school kids who sniff glue.

At times like this, I think about Granddad, and how he would have handled the situation. Granddad, taking a Bombay martini from a servant at his shooting lodge near Easton on Maryland's eastern shore, or Granddad, surveying his estate on the Hudson River through the window of his private railway car, or Granddad at his usual table at Le Pavillon, would—as I now recall—tell me not to worry about small things. "Life will straighten itself out," he liked to say. "As long as I'm here, as long as the people at the Morgan Guaranty Trust Company are there to look after things, only worry about what you want to worry about."

When I think about Granddad, I get a sense of peace and security. It does a lot to tide me over the rough patches here in Hollywood. Many other writers here might get worried about money, or about their careers being stuck in "park," or about how they are going to pay the rent in the future. But with Granddad and the folks at the Trust Department, I know everything will be all right.

I called Alex to tell her the bad news about the TV movie, and then to remind her about how Granddad so often would pause during a flight on his Gulfstream III to his private island near the Bahamas and remind us of how dicey building the railroad was, or how uncertain things looked when he had the telephone utility, or how many times things looked bleak at his own granddad's textile mills and steamship lines.

"Yes," Alex agreed with a sigh. "Granddad."

"He's a great comfort," I said.

"Yes, yes indeed."

"I've forgotten, by the way, what his name was."

"Chauncey," Alex reminded me. "Chauncey Denman Stein. He was both of our Granddads, in case you forgot."

"How could I ever forget anything about Granddad?"

MARCH 18, 1986

Did I tell you that my wife has a new job? Well, she does. She is now officially vice president for legal affairs at United Artists. Pretty hot stuff if you ask me. She works in a big building on Roxbury Drive. She has a car allowance. We picked out a shiny old Mercedes coupe for her. It's great. She works every night until about eleven and has to be at work at eight. She comes home so tired she can hardly open the door of the new Mercedes UA has bought for her—on time, of course.

In the meantime, I lie in bed reading a biography of Samuel Johnson.

"All that is needed to compel enmity is to excel."

"To confess envy is to confess superiority."

"A vacant mind is less displeased if the body is in constant motion and exercise."

"The safest and surest cure for misery is employment."

"Life is far more to be endured than to be enjoyed."

When Alex gets home, we have diet pizza or leftover fried chicken and read the Bible. I'm not kidding. Then we go to sleep, because Alex has to be up early the next day for meetings.

MARCH 19, 1986

Did I tell you that someone threw a brick through the window of my Porsche two Saturdays ago? While it was in the carport? It's the sixth time the car has been vandalized in the three years I've owned it. Usually the radio gets taken as well, but this time it was left, albeit damaged.

The Porsche dealership, owned by the kindly play-by-play man, NFL fullback, TV priest, and FTD "Tickler" huckster, does not have a window for it. Neither does any Porsche supply dump in America. They have to order it from Germany. It will take at least one month.

Plus, my Peugeot, the car we bought to transport the dogs, is completely broken. No air-conditioning, brakes shot, no dashboard lights. It's great. Basically I have no car any longer. I have two cars for which I paid more than fifty thousand dollars and neither of them can carry me one inch in any better style than if I had a fifteen-year-old Datsun van.

What better, more sharply etched confession of the complete bankruptcy of my life could there be than the state of my automobiles? In Los Angeles, where I, my very own self, said that "you are what you drive," I have no car. I am nothing. Or rather, I am a broken something.

I long to start afresh, to symbolically repair to a desert island and begin my life anew. That means maybe getting a Toyota Cressida, which is what Jude Wanniski, the famous supply-side guru, suggested to me ten years ago. You were right, Jude. A nice little Cressida. Very sturdy. Won't break. Won't attract attention. That would be perfect, thank you.

From now on, I'll let the newcomers have the Porsches and Mercedes and Jaguars and the ten-thousand-dollar-per-year repair bills. For me, a little cottage in the Cotswolds, a few teenage girls to come visit me and tell me about their lives, and maybe a burgundy Toyota Cressida. Every so often my wife will look in from United Artists and maybe let me drive her new Mercedes. And, of course, Granddad will stop by with his special yacht that can also go on land, and converts to a private railroad car.

To be fair, the broken cars are not an unmixed curse. Now that I have no car, I compel Sara to drive me all around town. Today she drove me to the doctor so I could complain about the L.A. flu. The doctor whistled at Sara and told me there was nothing I could do about the L.A. flu.

On the way home, Sara and I stopped at a fast-food Chinese place called Chin-Chin on the Sunset Strip. It was jammed with thin, trendy, angry-looking women in Esprit clothes. They looked up from their cold Chinese noodles at me and sneered. Then their glance strayed to Sara, walking next to me, and their jaws dropped open. Sara is so beautiful that men literally walk into the wall staring at her, and women visibly grimace at her youthful perfection.

Then the men and women look back at me and wonder.

We sat at the counter and watched recent Chinese emigrants make shu-mai, dumplings, vegetables in rice, and cilantro chicken. I started to quiz Sara about China. Did she know where China was? No. Did she know we had fought against China in a war? No. Had she ever heard of the Korean war? No. Had she ever heard of Korea? No. Had she ever heard of World War I? No. World War II? No. Franklin Delano Roosevelt? Ha! Surprise! She did know that one.

We ate the dumplings for a few minutes and then Sara said, "Ick. I don't like these. They taste like dog food."

So we left Chin-Chin and went back out onto the Strip. The

thin women sneered at me again, looked at Sara again, and reappraised me.

Fuck all the stuff about the Korean war. "Mankind shares a common doom"—Samuel Johnson said that—and while I have some time before doomsday, I want to spend it next to a beautiful girl walking in the sunshine down Sunset Strip with men walking into walls just looking at Sara and rich, thin women wondering what the hell is going on.

MARCH 20, 1986

A big news day, as John Chancellor used to say.

First, *Krypto*, AKA *Amerika*, has been fully revived, and I even got a small check this morning.

Second, I had lunch with a fascinating producer named Bob H. He had read a series I wrote for the *Herald* about mistresses and he wanted to option television rights. He also said he had seen me walking along the beach at Malibu with Mary, my late dog.

We rendezvoused at The Palm, which used to be my daily lunchtime hangout. Now The Palm looks eerily unfamiliar, maniacally cheerful, filled with plump, happy faces. Those faces once looked to me like the essence of what I wanted from Hollywood. Now they look to me as if they have been divorced from real life for ten years, sent to a farm to be fattened up, and now they are down here to be slaughtered, only they don't know it yet.

Ted was a corpulent man in his mid-fifties with a vaguely wild, out-of-control look on his face. "I grew up all by myself," he said. "My father abandoned my mother when I was two years old. I don't even know who my grandparents were. I dropped out of school in sixth grade, but I'm completely self-educated. My former wife went to Cheltenham Ladies College, that famous girls' school in England where the daughters of the Queen go, and she can trace her ancestry back a thousand years. So go figure. I'm on a diet," Ted said. "So I'm only gonna have half a steak. Whadda you want?"

"I'll have the other half of your steak."

"Nahh, I have to take that home to have for lunch tomorrow," Ted said.

"Okay. I'll have roast beef hash."

"You know what I drive?" Ted asked. "An Aston Martin. A convertible. I have to pick it up at the dealer for repairs this afternoon. You know what it'll cost?"

"A million dollars."

"Thirty-three hundred dollars. Last time it was eleven thousand dollars. Just for a tune-up."

"Wow."

"So listen, I think we can do some business on this mistress thing. Whadda ya think?"

"I think so."

"You know," he said, "I've done a lot of shows. Westerns. Detective shows. Every kind of show. And I'm not afraid of the network. The network is just one scared guy worrying whether he'll have his job on Friday."

"You're right there."

"So I can pick this thing up and ram it down their throats. Plus, I've been thinking I'd like to do a series about a detective in Washington. Like you. From a really establishment Washington family. You think you'd like to work on that?"

"You bet."

"So whadda you want out of life?" he asked me. "Seriously."

My heart sank. That was the con man's line of the year. It had just replaced, "Now tell me, Benjy, what can I possibly do for you to make your life easier?" Also usually punctuated with "Seriously."

"I'd like to spend my whole life suing people who have screwed me over," I answered. "That and appear on TV."

"Great," Ted said. "Ya know what I'd like?"

"A Toyota?"

"Naah. I'd like to move to the South of France, and just lie there on the beach and have everyone know I was so rich that they were all crazy, and I'd be lying there one day and two beautiful fifteen-year-old girls would come by and one would say to the other, 'Who's that funny-looking fat guy on the beach?' And the other girl would say, 'I hear he's a very rich American who gets a lot of money every week from Hollywood.' And the first girl would say, 'You know, he's kind of cute.'"

I looked at Ted and felt thoroughly sad.

Ted looked at me. Abruptly, his whole face seemed to dissolve and he stared at his steak remnant. "So? So what am I supposed to do?"

"I don't know," I said.

Ted looked totally confused. I gave him a copy of my book, inscribed "For Ted, who has been on his own since he was fourteen."

By the time I got home, I had an obsolete *New York Times* with a long obituary of Bernard Malamud. I have always loved him, ever since I read *Dubin's Lives* and could just feel the anguish that poor schlemiel writer felt when he saw his co-ed girlfriend balling that gondolier in their hotel room in Venice, the little bitch. That was only a few years after I moved to L.A. The idea that a man could fall madly in love was real to me. The idea that a man could be severely hurt by a woman's casual infidelity was likewise vivid and excruciating, although I am usually the one dishing it out and not the one taking it. I tracked down Malamud somewhere in New England and sent him a copy of *'Ludes*, and he sent me a wonderful note, which I saved for five years, about how people could see the same sorrow and the same delusion whether they were in Hollywood or Vermont.

Now, time has passed. I can hardly believe I ever felt moved at stories of infidelity. After ten years in Hollywood, I cannot believe that any man cares enough about any woman to really worry about whether or not she fucks the gondolier. For Christ's sake, that man might better use the time calling his Italian distributor and checking on European receipts for a picture. He might be getting an incredible European delivery price on a Ferrari. He might be getting custom-made shoes on the Via Condotti in Rome.

Well, maybe that's going too far. I guess I can imagine married people, like me or like my friend Al, caring about our wives. I know my pal Sid has not walked fully upright since his wife died three years ago. Frankly, I haven't really felt right since his wife died three years ago. But we are dinosaurs, foolish and sentimental Tories of emotion in the free market Whig world of L.A.

I wonder what Malamud would have made of the perpetual souk that is Los Angeles. I suspect it would have made him think of his father, who was worried—and with reason—about getting yelled at for giving a stick of butter to a starving woman. I think that Malamud might have understood the world of material lavishness and emotional Gramm-Rudman that is Los Angeles.

I sat out by the pool for a long time and watched the dogs play on the flagstone in the sun. BMWs and Porsches and ancient battered Cadillacs sped by, absolutely without regard to the small children playing a few feet away.

What would Bernard Malamud have made of this fact: that I never hear men talking about being in love, and I mean *never*, but I often hear about what great blow jobs different women give. What would Malamud, who felt every quiver of human feeling the way a seismometer in Pasadena feels a small tremor in Ceylon, feel about the Krakatoa of human isolation and misery that values servility and skill and does not even make a market in connection and feelings between men and women?

Well, there's no money in thinking about that, so I went upstairs to watch TV. I snapped the remote control and watched *Divorce Court*. It was about a couple who became addicted to Percodan. Hmmm.

Better skip that.

Snap.

A replay of Mr. T. about white slavery in Kansas.

Snap

Amadeus, but a boring part.

Snap.

A seminar about buying property with no money down.

Snap.

A sitcom about a black gynecologist teaching his daughter to ride a bicycle.

Snap.

A grinning fool with a wig talking about the weather.

Snap.

An advertisement promising that if I buy a certain kind of truck, my future as ladies' man is assured.

Snap, snap, and snap, and now the TV is off and I can go back to reading about Samuel Johnson.

You see, this is the problem with L.A. life. I have the best TV Sony makes, with remote fucking control. But there's nothing to watch.

Granddad would understand.

MARCH 23, 1986

Have I told you about my pal from high school, Tammie? She is a little pistol who sits across from me. She is tall, with blue eyes and black hair and a perpetually waiflike, faraway look. She almost never pays attention in class. She does eat huge candy bars while she reads Jackie Susann novels. I have been talking to her after class for a few months now, and I have learned that her parents are divorced. Her father is a physicist. Her mother is a broker. Tammie lives with Mom.

When I first started having these little tête-à-têtes with

Tammie, she told me that she does not plan to go to college. She planned to become an accountant. But now that I have been paying attention to her, she wants to go to college. In fact, she wants to do what I should have done if I'd had any sense. She wants to become a historian.

When I stand out in the parking lot at Birmingham High School and see how much Tammie has blossomed since I began to tell her she has a future, I feel about as good as anything in L.A. makes me feel. First, I am in high school. My feeble, confused brain thinks that means I am young again, so that's a plus. Then again, I am standing there with a cute little five-foot-tall pixie with black hair who listens carefully to every word I say. That's worth something. Third, this child's life will almost certainly change—and drastically—for the better if I can, so to speak, have my way with her about going to college.

It's Easter vacation at Birmingham High School, so I haven't seen Tammie for a while. I called her this morning to ask if she wanted to have lunch with me. "I'm not gonna be around for lunch," she said in her prematurely deep voice. "How about dinner?"

We met at Morton's. She wore black trousers and a sweater with spangly things on it. She looked *fabulous*. She got there before I did, and the waiters had already brought her two glasses of wine.

We talked for a long time about her old boyfriend, a major punk rock musician named "Tractor Trailer" and how badly he had treated poor little Tammie. Then we talked about Tammie's new boyfriend, a stereo repairman named Tommy. "It's a secret," Tammie confided, "but on my eighteenth birthday next month, Tommy and I are going to get engaged."

"You're kidding. What about college?"

"Well, I can still go to college," Tammie said. "At Cal State Northridge, maybe, or UCLA."

"I thought maybe I could help you get into Barnard, or maybe Wellesley."

"What's Barnard?"

"Never mind. It's a very good college in New York City. In the meantime, tell me what drugs you like to take."

"I don't take any drugs," Tammie said. "That's a cliché about teenagers that's not true."

"Hah. I have never known a teenager who does not take drugs, and you will not be the first." This is an L.A. way of making conversation.

"It's true," she said. "I don't take drugs."

"I'll bet."

"Look," Tammie said. "There are all kinds of clichés about older men, too. I mean, like old men are supposed to only want to go out with young girls like me so you can sleep with us. Is that true?"

"Objection. No foundation."

"Well, see. That's a cliché, too, just like your clichés about me and drugs."

By this time, Tina Sinatra was looking over at us and laughing. "She has a point," Tina said from the next table.

I strolled out of the room to go to the men's room and think of what else I could tell Tammie about college. At the second round table was a familiar figure. Ron Meyer, superagent and Hollywood mover and shaker, was there with one of his clients, a guy named Sylvester Stallone. Ron called me over to the table.

"Ben," he said, "do you know Sly Stallone?"

"I haven't had the pleasure," I said. "But I did once tell the correspondent from Izvestia that you were a creative genius, when he called you a war monger."

"You did that for me?" Sly said in his best "Yo, Adrian" voice.

"Yes, because I think you are a creative genius," I said. "A real one."

"Jeez," he said, "thanks."

I felt a tugging at my sleeve. Tammie had appeared at my side. "Sly," I said brazenly, "this is my friend Tammie."

"How are you?" Sly said, looking friendly. "You enjoyin' yourself?"

"Yes I am," she said straightforwardly.

When we got back to the table, Tammie was so excited she could hardly control herself. "I can't wait to tell Tommy and Cathy and all my friends that I met Sly Stallone," she said.

In the parking lot, while the valet brought around Tammie's Volkswagen and my Peugeot (it's fixed but the Porsche is still broken), she said, "This was the best dinner I've ever had. I would love to come back here."

And I would love to take you, little sylph.

MARCH 25, 1986

A telephone call from the Cable News Network. They want me to appear on *Larry King Live* with Geraldo Rivera and talk about the sexual harassment of starlets in Hollywood. Sounds right to me. I am never too tired to appear on TV. What else is there to make you feel as if you were immortal than to appear on a little piece of videotape stuck away in a library until it rots?

Also, Tammie was due to come over to receive instruction in how to write an essay to help her get into college. She was also ready to start working with me on organizing my files of articles. This, I cheerfully assured her, would help her get into college. After all, what could be a better credit than an after-school job working for a journalist who had actually once written speeches for Richard Nixon and had met him many times?

Tammie appeared at the door just as Sara was telling me in unbelievable detail about how her boyfriend had made her cut her hair a new way. Sara's hair always looks as if it has received more attention than the North American Air Defense Command, but I try not to think much about it.

I conducted Tammie into my labyrinthine, overwhelming files. I showed her dozens of drawers of articles about everything from TV comedy to antitrust to mergers and acquisitions. She looked terrified.

"Maybe this isn't right for you," I said. "How about coming to watch me appear on TV instead?"

She liked that idea much better. At the CNN studio on Sunset Boulevard, I talked to New York and to Geraldo while Tammie flirted with a sound engineer. When we got off the show, she said, "Cheeze, that guy was really flirting with me. I can't imagine why he would do such a thing, can you, Mr. Stein?" She batted her eyes.

She also said she was hungry, and had I ever heard of a place called Spago?

And so, dinner at Spago, which was not at all noteworthy except that she told me I had become her guardian angel. After dinner, I took Tammie across the street to Tower Records. I took her down the endless brightly lit wide aisles, past the punks and the drug addicts, and bought her one little 45 of "What the World Needs Now." She hugged it to her chest and twirled around in the aisle. "This is wonderful, isn't it, Mr. Stein?" she asked. "I feel as if this is Christmas."

I took her home. Alex was just getting out of her new car. Tammie and Alex said hello to each other, and then Tammie had to leave to meet Tommy, her boyfriend, at the stereo store.

Alex has been convinced that I am completely insane for a long time now. She watched Tammie go, smiled, and started to tell me about her day at United Artists.

Late at night, Alex and the three dogs lay in bed asleep. Their rhythmic, unsynchronized breathing made the mattress rise and fall like the waters of a choppy small pond. I looked out at the lights of the Valley: Little Tammie hugging that 45 of "What the World Needs Now" to her breast, twirling in the bright wide aisle at Tower Records, saying, "Gee, Mr. Stein, this is just like Christmas." Oh, you sweet, sweet child.

April 3, 1986

Dinner at Morton's with Lucinda DeMott. The night before, she finished taping a new pilot with Alan King. "It was great," she said. "Alan King married to Dina Merrill, so it's got a lot of laughs from the start. You can see that, can't you?"

"Of course I can," I said.

In the front of the room at the first square table sat Lee Rich. He came over to Lucinda and kissed her repeatedly. He made a gesture of sparring with me. Lee is the main stockholder of Lorimar. He is about as rich as any Rockefeller. Why shouldn't he be? The Rockefellers only brought oil to industrial Amerika. Lee Rich invented *Dallas* and *Falcon Crest*.

I really have a hard time eating at Morton's any longer. I see all the rich men and women, the movie stars, the studio executives, the agents, the power-lawyers, and I have nothing in common with them. Some part of what Hollywood means has permanently escaped me. See, I can watch it, and appreciate the cathedrals of imagination and the swamps of idiocy, but I no longer feel connected to Hollywood. Too much aggravation. Too much bad luck. I am only a tourist here, and I am eager to move on to the next stop.

No, I'm not. Never mind.

April 4, 1986

This is life:

About ten days ago, I bought much more stock than I can afford. After all, the market gave every impression of rising forever. It had gone up to 1800 on the Dow in a few months from about 1300. Oil prices were falling, bringing down interest rates, making stocks look better every day.

I see in this morning's *Los Angeles Times* that in the last week, the Dow-Jones Industrial Average has fallen by 100 points. It's the largest one-week fall in history. Every stock I own has been hard hit. Blue chips like CBS down 15 points. Little dogs like Kingworld, down 10. My options on the S & P 100, virtually wiped off the map.

By this point, I have acquired a certain detachment. A whiz-kid seraph troublemaker is simply doing his job. It's his job to make me feel terrible, and it's my job to feel terrible.

"Life," said Samuel Johnson, "is far more to be endured than to be enjoyed." He was not wrong, but he did not go far enough. But then, he did not know what it's like to have the radio stolen out of his Porsche six times in two years or to have options on the S & P 100.

A telephone call from my mother. "Did you know that we have Faeroe ants?" she asked. "They're so small that when you see them marching across the counter looking for food, you're not even sure you're seeing them. They're about as long as a straightpin is wide. But, if you can believe this, when you look at them, they get so scared they stop. They know you're looking at them." My mother sighed over the long distance telephone from the Watergate in Washington, D.C. "Life," she said, and that made me start to cry, so I hung up the phone.

Then a telephone call from H., my pal who works on *Miami Vice*. "So I'm doing this video with Michael Jackson," he says, "and I go over to his house in Encino to talk to him, and I'm sitting talking to him, and this chimpanzee in a silk tuxedo, only chimpanzee size, jumps out of a chandelier and lands on my lap, and just sits on my lap the whole time I'm talking to Michael Jackson, and Michael Jackson starts giggling and says, 'Oooh, you're so lucky. He really *likes* you, and he hardly *likes* anybody.' So my guess is that Michael Jackson probably is gonna set off onto that monkey's ear now that it's touched me."

"You're a vain guy," I said.

"I know what I'm worth," H. said. "By the way, everybody's been fired off *Miami Vice*. You think you'd like to work on it next season?"

"I don't think so," I said.

"Well, I probably can't get you the gig anyway. I'm not sure you have network clearance."

After Alex went to sleep, I drove out onto Outpost Drive, past Jackson Browne's house, past Gore Vidal's house, past Harrison Ford's house, and onto the glittery bright nighttime world of La Brea Boulevard. A woman with a halter top and spangled jeans beckoned to me in my car. Two men in a Cadillac were parked in front of a liquor store madly smoking a huge joint. Six Marines with jarhead haircuts wandered down the street, following two swivel-hipped Filipino hookers with no front teeth. In front of the Carl's, Jr., a black man in rags screamed that white people had put radar in his brain. A woman with an absolutely immobile mask of rage and anger sat at the wheel of a white Rolls-Royce convertible with the motor running inside the Mayfair Market parking lot. She had to be at least seventy years old, and I would back her against Leon Spinks any day. A punk boy and girl, both with heads shaved, walked past the Scientology center playing a huge ghetto blaster belting out "Strawberry Fields Forever."

I turned around at a store run by Afghan refugees and parked the car. Inside the store, I bought a copy of the new *Fortune* to see if I could learn how to win at investing. I didn't even bother to read it. I just threw in onto the floor of the Peugeot. Just the thought of *Fortune*, with its neat charts of per-share earnings, at a newsstand in a store run by Afghan refugees, catering mostly to black hookers patronized by Iranian used-car salesmen who share the girls with gun-toting pimps, is unbearable, insane. Any form of orderliness in the context of Hollywood by night is a joke, like wearing a dinner jacket to the riots at Attica.

When I got home, I watched the lights of Universal far below.

The Santa Ana was picking up, blowing pine needles into the pool again. The pool filter is broken. That's another thing.

Not only that, but I just read in *The Wall Street Journal* that the Department of Transportation is recalling about ten billion Toyotas. Their cruise control is broken. The Cressida is liable to suddenly go from stop into passing gear and run over ten children in front of a school. That just happened in Anaheim.

What's the solution? The Movie Channel is showing *Blade Runner*. You can't ask for more than that. Daryl Hannah doing six hand-flips through the air, then choking Harrison Ford with her thighs before he blasts her with his ray gun. Far out.

April 6, 1986

Forget all that whining. Forget all that crap about Samuel Johnson. Everything's coming up night-blooming jasmine.

First, the stock market was up 37 points today. So you see, I was right to hold on to my stock after all. Of course, the ones I sold, like Disney, did better than the ones I held on to, but still, you see the point. I finally did something right.

Second, a call from my agent, a handsome young kid named Robb. "We have four offers for that story you wrote about the hookers at USC," he said. "So we're off to the races. We might get a few bucks for that one."

When he says "few" he means it, but still, it's better than a humiliating pass, which is what I usually get.

Third, I appeared on the George Putnam radio show this morning. George is a bluff, hearty guy who is supposedly the prototype for Ted Baxter on the old *Mary Tyler Moore Show*. He is right on every single issue—he loves Israel, digs Reagan, most of all adores animals of all kinds. I love the guy.

We had call-ins from every corner of the greater Los Angeles metroplex. One elderly lady after another called to say how much she loved my columns in the *Herald,* then how much she loved hearing me on the radio, and what a buff guy I was. "You know, if I were younger, I'd like to have Mr. Stein stay at my apartment for a weekend," said one caller. "If you know what I mean."

"I know what you mean, darling," George Putnam said.

As soon as I got home, there was an urgent call to appear on *Crossfire,* a CNN show with angry people arguing with each other. My job was to argue against Robert "Baretta" Blake about the so-called Great Peace March. I showed up at the studio in my brown wool suit from Paul Stuart. Blake showed up wearing cut-off jeans, a T-shirt, and a pink sweat band. I told Blake that I thought the Great Peace March was an exercise in banality.

"Don't say that, man," he said. "You're a better person than that. You have some spiritual qualities."

"This man is not well," I opined, but I think the microphone was turned off.

Robert Novak, in Washington, asked Blake if he planned to see the president that weekend. Blake enthusiastically nodded yes. "But the president's in Santa Barbara for a week," Novak crowed.

"I know Ronald Reagan a lot better than you do. I used to work with him on *Death Valley Days,*" Blake said proudly.

I asked Blake if he would take his march all the way to Moscow, like Napoleon. "Be quiet," he said. "Your mother raised you better than that. You should be ashamed of your bad self."

Just as I was about to step into the elevator, I had another call in the control room.

"Mr. Stein, you should do a show about what older men want to do to little girls like me. They look at me and they have all kinds of ideas about how they'd like to get their hands on us, and then they'd get us pregnant, and they'd really like that, but they can't do it. It's not allowed, no matter how much they'd like to do it."

"Marcie? How did you get this number?"

"I like to call in programs," she said. "I got fired at the Burger Ballroom."

"Thanks for your attention," I said.

"Lissen," she asked, "when can we get together? I have a lot of stories to tell you."

"Any day now."

I went down to the garage and got my Porsche. It's running again, with a new window and a very cheap stereo. I have to put a sign in the window whenever I park it. The sign says NOT A BLAUPUNKT—CHEAP STEREO—NOT WORTH STEALING. Not too cool, but it might save me the cost of a new window.

At home the pool was warm. I swam for half an hour, and then Tammie came over to have me help her write her essay to get into college. She sank into a chair and I gave her a cookie. She ate the cookie and looked up at me. "I'm not sure Tommy and I are going to get engaged after all," she said. "Maybe we'll wait a little while."

She looked up at me with her big blue eyes and smiled. She wore a retainer. "Do you have any milk?" she asked. "I like to have cookies with milk."

APRIL 11, 1986

A frantic telephone call from my sister, a housewife, writer, and fund-raiser in New York. "Have you seen *The Wall Street Journal* this morning?" she demanded.

Oh, Christ. "No. Is the stock exchange folding?"

"Worse. You know that L.A. flu you're always talking about?"

"Yes."

"Well, apparently it leads to incurable cancer. You'd better read the article."

With shaking hands, I read the article. My sister had it wrong. *If,* and only *if,* I have a certain kind of virus, and *if* and only *if* I have it long enough, it can turn into cancer of the nose. Thank you, sister.

Still, I felt scared. What if this L.A. flu is only the prelude to worse? Far stranger things have happened. Far stranger things have happened to me. I sat through all of *Invasion U.S.A.*, frightened, even terrified.

I went to the kitchen. The dogs jumped up and down and begged for a dog biscuit. I gave Martha, Trixie, and Ginger one each. In the precise dish with her name on it.

Sara came bounding through the door and asked me if I liked her hair in its new way. The telephone rang. It was the local distributor of *Her Only Sin* wanting to know if lunch was all set at The Palm. It was.

The phone rang again. Tammie wanted to tell me that I was her guardian angel, and would I like to be a chaperon at her senior prom? "Really, Mr. Stein, all the kids from class want you to come."

Elena ironed in the guest room while she watched Spanish-language TV telling her about U.S. carriers off Libya. Let's play Global Thermonuclear War!

I read fan letters from the *Herald-Examiner.* "Thank God for a man who sees the threats to America the way you do."

"Too bad Hitler didn't get you, you stinking Jew kike."

My usual run of letters, in other words.

My Porsche started right up. I took down its sign reading CHEAP STEREO—NOT WORTH STEALING and went on my way. The sun was dazzling, lighting up every tall blade of dried grass along Mulholland Drive, even shooting reflections off the surf at Redondo Beach, almost fifty miles away. There were almost no other cars on the road. Even on Outpost, the sun sent spokes of dusty light through the oak trees against the smooth stucco of the Spanish colonial revival houses, and no other cars, or even pedestrians, were there to distract me from the light.

Down at the bottom of Outpost, at La Brea, normal daily life resumed. A fat blond woman leaned against the side of a light blue Volvo station wagon. Its driver's door had just been torn off by a huge, rusting Buick Electra. The driver of the Buick sat stock still in the driver's seat, tears rolling down his cheeks. The blond woman was methodically writing notes in her Day-Timer.

Farther down La Brea, a new hooker had appeared in a red satin skirt. She actually looked scared. I paused at the corner of Hollywood and La Brea and examined her face. She still had some alertness, some slight willingness to please, to be psychically involved in the world around her about her eyes. Her teeth were white and even. She winked at a young kid in a pickup truck with a surfboard in the back. He pulled over and she got into the car.

At The Palm, there was frantic noise, as always. Don Petrone, major entertainment legal honcho, sat with another lawyer. Marvin Worth, who produces movies like *Lenny,* sat in a dark booth laughing at a man's jokes. A young man and woman who were respectively a Xerox operator and a typist when I came here ten years ago and are now a producer and a casting agent fed themselves great heaps of salad and smiled at the passersby.

A waiter named Carlo asked me whether the time was right to buy real estate. The bartender, Rico, asked me what I thought about Robert Blake. "I'm sure he's a good family man," I said.

The distributor appeared. He had been a neighbor of mine in Maryland, long ago, when he had played basketball at the University of Maryland. "That was before the school was integrated, wasn't it?" I asked.

"Of course." He laughed. "Otherwise I wouldn't even have gotten on the bench."

We ate hash and fish, and the distributor asked me if I missed being at Yale. "Of course I miss it," I said. "Those were palmy days. Great days. Wonderful days. To be young and involved in the struggle for what we thought would be a better world. To be young and get so much attention. Just to be young."

He nodded enthusiastically.

" 'Twas bliss in that day to be alive, but to be young was very heaven," said Wordsworth, and you know what, Bill? It wasn't just in the days of the Vendée, but in the days of Abbie and Bobby and Jerry and Jimi and Janis. I thought about all of that era, the rallies on the New Haven Green, the late nights talking about revolution, the years when we thought we would be forever young, when there was music in the cafés at night and revolution in the air, when we thought we could live forever in fun, but our chances really were a million to one.

It was a magical time. Magic. No two ways about it. I zoomed along Santa Monica Freeway and drifted off into the past. It was magic then—I recalled—because we knew that anything could happen. In the next demonstration we might get clubbed, or we might bring the troops home. At the next screening of *Battle of Algiers* to raise money for the Black Panther party, we might meet a blond girl with the face of an angel who did not want to be alone that night. We might tell the teacher of antitrust that he was a bully and become a folk hero of the law school. Oh, happy day, and now so long ago.

Since my job is to draw conclusions and make comparisons, one of them suddenly dropped on me out of the blue, like a speeding ticket. You might think that Hollywood, with its hustling and lying and money-grubbing, is about as different from a "free Bobby Seale rally" as you can get. Yes, you might think that, but then you would be wrong.

The essence of Hollywood is exactly the same: it is a launching pad into the realms of anything can happen. It is Cape Canaveral for trips to a new, wildly bigger, more important, more powerful you. In that sense, Hollywood has *precisely* the same magic as New Haven in 1969.

A layer of possibility that the little thought I had while I was getting the car washed can and will wind up on a silver screen sixty feet wide by forty feet high hangs over the concrete facts of the day like the haze which overlays the city in June. That haze seeps into every detail, into every pore of the actual, so that the trip to the grocery store can be the start of a story that will be a script and will make me rich beyond avarice, and express a basic truth that people need to know. That fog of usually, *but not always*, vain potential makes every day the optional beginning of immortality on the big and small screen.

It does not matter that the dream is so rarely—if ever—made actual. The point is that the dream is always there, mixing seamlessly with the real, so that no one truly in the business knows where the fact ends and the fantasy begins. That is the glory of Los Angeles life—the ineluctable mingling of what is and what could be if life were a dream.

Those sixties and early seventies days in New Haven and Washington and Santa Cruz had that same dreamlike feel: *anything can happen, we have slipped the moorings of the probable.* On a good day here, these days blend into the days of Free All Political Prisoners. All of my life seems to be a sunny meadow of potential, rising over the nagging details of broken cars and income tax audits and losing stock market gambles. This is a business for most of the successful people in it. For me, it is a room to dream in. And, incredibly, sometimes the dreams really do come true.

Now home to do some work. The bills are real.

APRIL 18, 1986

Lunch today at The Ivy with Bobbie Leigh Zito. About three weeks ago, I was on a radio talk show. We talked about Hollywood, about child molestation, about animals. A listener called in from her car phone. She was the wife of a successful director of Chuck Norris movies: *Missing in Action, Invasion U.S.A.*, you get the picture. She and her husband had met when they were starving students at City College. Now they make more money than they know what to do with, so they spend some of it on cellular telephone calls. That's Bobbie Leigh Zito.

We argued on the radio, but then she wrote me a fan letter at the *Herald-Examiner* and invited me to lunch. I rarely get invited to lunch by strange women, or make that "women I don't already know." But Bobbie Leigh sounded like a character, so off I went to The Ivy.

The Ivy is located smack in the middle of the worst aura part of Los Angeles—West Hollywood, in the middle of all the interior design studios and the fabric wholesalers. Hardened, cruel-looking women driving Jaguars race in and out of showrooms all day long looking as if they are being pursued by the hounds of hell. Someday I would love to give the Minnesota Multiphasic Personality Inventory to a randomly selected group of women with ASID cards. I suspect the results would frighten Curtis LeMay. I'm going to assign Sara to find out if there are any articles on the differences in levels of aggression and hostility between women interior designers and other people.

My big dread whenever I meet new people is that they will turn out to be grossly fat and insane-looking. Fifteen years ago, a woman called my phone number by mistake when I was working as a poverty lawyer. She told me she was a nude model, and not only that, but was used as a canvas for body-painting. I invited her to my office. She showed up a week later, a blimp with severe acne. Ever since then, I have been afraid that she would find my address.

Bobbie Leigh Zito was not only slender and pretty, but had a sweet face. In The Ivy, with its full complement of toughened Hollywood types hunched conspiratorially over their crabcakes, she was a little purple flower of sweetness. Also funny. Also smart.

"I think I saw you once on that American flight twenty-one to New York," she said.

"I think you probably did," I agreed. "I hope I wasn't reading the trades. There's nothing in the whole world less cool than reading the trades on the airplane to New York."

"My husband, Joe-Joe, has a great idea for that flight," Bobbie said. "On the flight east, it'll be traffic school for people who got speeding tickets. On the way west, it'll be Coke-Enders. Why waste the time?"

"Makes perfect sense to me."

We talked about the life of Hollywood and about our pasts. "I used to be a schoolteacher in Harlem," she said. "The kids were all black and the teachers were all Jewish, so there was a lot of racial tension in the air. One day I had this little sixth-grader named Tuna Fish Johnson. He wore a porkpie hat to class every day. He had already done time in juvenile hall for robbing a grocery store at lunchtime. So I told him he had to take off his hat in class.

"'I can't take it off,' he said.

"'Why not?' I asked him.

"''Cause I'm Jewish,' Tuna Fish said.

"'You're not Jewish or else you'd know how to read,' I told him, and then word of it got back to the school board and they told me I was a racist and fired me," Bobbie Leigh said.

"God, weren't the sixties great?"

"Tin soldiers and Nixon's coming." We gave each other a soul shake and a finger shake.

Horrible deep bass music came over the "sound system" of The Ivy. I asked the captain if he could turn it down. "I'm sorry," he said. "Miss Von Kersting insists that it play at a certain volume and she locks the volume control so I can't touch it."

Incredible. In L.A., in New York, on airplanes, everywhere, mankind is bombarded with horrible, brain-damaging music. You cannot go into an elevator or a men's room or a drugstore without hearing ghastly, sickening deep bass music pounding at your brain. Where did the idea come from that it was cool to have loud music attacking you in every public place? Who in his right mind enjoys such horrors? I once read that loud rock music, especially bass, breaks up brain waves and makes it impossible to concentrate. I see it all the time. Even secretaries listen to music at their desks. And they can't think. The whole nation listens to horrible deep bass and then goes out and elects Reagan. Our parents were right after all. Rock 'n' roll *is* a plot and ruins our brains.

Still, we carried on. Bobbie Leigh told me about her neighborhood, then asked me if I had any good scripts. I looked her right in her deep green eyes, "No," I said. "What's a script?"

Bobbie Leigh had a sweet, adorable quality to her. Talking about scripts with someone like her would be like asking the cerebral palsy poster girl who her agent is.

The room was filled with celebrities. David Geffen was having lunch with John Kolodner, a powerful A & R man in the music business who works for Geffen. James Coburn was having lunch with a pretty middle-aged woman. He looks like he is stuck together with airplane glue. Then there was some character actor who struck it rich by getting a part on *The A-Team*. Then a beautiful woman with a purple knit dress. I think she is a call girl for wealthy airplane dealers. So you see. Many celebrities indeed.

Bobbie Leigh and I finished our lunch and walked out into the air. For the last few days, brutal Santa Anas have blown through the L.A. basin each night. The results are palm fronds in our pool, downed electrical wires, umbrellas blowing through restaurant windows, and clear sharp sunny days. There is a hint of a chill mixed with perfect, cloudless skies and eighty-degree temperatures. Everyone looks happy, on edge, anticipating something great. I bid Bobbie Leigh good-bye and went to Beverly Hills to take a walk.

For the first time in months, I thought that I will probably never live in the East again. Why should I? If there are people like Bobbie Leigh, perfect days, and my goddess wife all here, why go anywhere else? Unless . . . unless I found a place where there was a law against playing loud music outside the home. That would be the Garden of Eden.

APRIL 19, 1986

I should really have told you about Trixie before now. She is my favorite, my dream dog, my lover hound angel.

Almost fifteen years ago, when I was teaching at the University of California at Santa Cruz, my hippie girlfriend and I decided we should have a dog. At first we wanted an Irish setter. But before we could even start to look for a setter, fate intervened. One morning we heard a loud, ghostly howl from outside our apartment. I opened the door and saw there an enormous Weimaraner, gray and gorgeous, baying at the morning sun. I opened the door for the Weimaraner. He ran into our apartment—on the first floor—jumped up onto our bed, and promptly fell asleep.

I named him Hirohito. Alas, two days later, his owner, a leader of a feminist antisexism collective, came by and picked him up.

The very next day, my girlfriend and I answered an advertisement in the *Chronicle* for Weimaraner puppies. We drove all the way to San Francisco, found the address of a small house in Daly City, and had our pick of puppies.

We chose a little female hiding under a couch because she had the biggest paws. We carried her home in my little blue Subaru to our apartment with my girlfriend holding her on her lap in a napkin.

It was love at first sight. Mary slept in my long, down-to-there hair, followed after me when I walked to class, even curled up inside my jacket while I watched movies. She was a warm ball of perfection in a chaotic world.

Mary and I were inseparable for ten years. She lived with me in Santa Cruz, then in a tiny rented house in Georgetown, in my first owned house in Wesley Heights, then in a penthouse in Brooklyn Heights, a thirty-third-floor apartment on the West Side before it was hip, and then in my funky chateau in the Hollywood Hills. She lived with us when we were artists in Aspen, when we were beachcombers in Malibu, when we were recluses in Rancho Mirage.

She slept under the covers. She sucked my thumb when she was nervous, and fell asleep with it still clamped in her jaws. I loved her madly. She kept me company while I wrote, my only groupie, and more than enough at that.

My wife loved her, too, but it was I who had known her when she was small enough to hold in one hand while I typed with the other, I who had walked with her through the redwoods of Santa Cruz on stormy nights. The girlfriend was gone within a year. The dog stayed. The term "a man and his dog" is not just words.

For reasons known best to Him, God took my Mary to heaven on April 20, 1982. She had been fighting cancer for two years with chemo, radiation, and repeated surgery. The pain was tangible in her eyes, and so we sent her off to eternity, paralyzed, gaunt, but still my sacred angel.

It was the worst day of my life.

The very next day, we got a new Weimaraner from Animal Alliance, the people who take in lost and abandoned dogs and bring them to convalescent homes. She was a fine dog, much smaller than Mary, with a long tail and a permanently terrified look. She was good company, but she turned out to be from outer space.

For one thing, her tail got markedly longer and shorter depending upon the phases of the moon or whether she was inside or outside. For another, she routinely opened locked closets and removed food. She also could open my briefcase, take out papers, and lock up the briefcase again.

For still another, she ate all of the leather padding on the steering wheel, dashboard, and gearshift of my Mercedes coupe. She also refused to be left in a car. If you foolishly did so, she would release the parking brake and send it crashing into the car next to it.

This is Los Angeles, so we consulted a dog psychologist, who was just as much of a charlatan as you would expect. The crackpot suggested that we get her a dog to keep her company. We were desperate, so we agreed.

Two weeks later, Traci brought home from Animal Alliance the absolutely most beautiful animal I have ever seen. She was a spotted brown and white German short-haired pointer. Her white fur was ermine. Her brown was mink. Her coat was uniquely soft. Her snout was long and delicately tapered. Her eyes were perfect limpid pools of brown love. Her wagging white tail had a piquant tuft at its end.

When she first came to our house, she was so scared that her whole body shook. It was as if, in a desperate effort to please, she was wagging her whole self.

This glamorous waif had been the property of a surgeon in Encino, or so we were told. But the dog had supposedly howled when left outside, and the surgeon's wife had made him give up "Tiffany," which is about as perfect an Encino name as you are ever going to find. It's not a bad handle for a call girl, but out of the question for a vision of paradise. At my sacred wife's suggestion, we renamed her Trixie, which was meant to contrast with her obvious nobility.

Within a few days, Trixie was my special angel. She first slept with her head on the carpet near the bed. Then she slept half off and half on the bed. Then she slept next to me on the bed. The first morning that I awakened with Trixie pressed up next to me, I looked in her eyes and saw a look every man would love to see on a female face and few do.

The look said, "I am warm. I am innocent. I am giving. Do with me what you will."

A few words about what it feels like to have a soft, warm, flexible, furry Trixie pressed up against you while you lie in bed: An

Angel of the Lord has appeared to you and told you that you will live forever, that every day will bring peace of mind, comfort, warmth, and balmy breezes blowing in off Nassau Beach. You are in the center of the universe and nothing can harm you. Your life transcends struggle, fear, endings.

After that morning, Trixie was my girl. She followed me from room to room, would not eat unless I fed her (unless I was out of town), and slept on a ratty couch nearby while I wrote.

One night when I had insomnia, I got into the bed in the guest bedroom to watch *Rebecca*. Trixie jumped up and lay next to me. When I awoke in the morning, Trixie and I were the only ones in bed. She yawned and leaned into me more languidly than ever.

From that night on, Trixie would beckon to me each night at bedtime to get into the guest bed with her. As I went through the house turning off lights and locking doors, Trixie would jump onto the guest bed, yawn ostentatiously, make loud sighs, and wag her whole self.

Her message was simple: Get in bed with me, you fool, instead of that wife of yours, sacred though she may be.

I have to confess that on many nights, the allure worked. I would get into bed with my innocent wife. She would fall asleep over an open Barbara Pym. I would cover her with the blankets, turn out the light, and creep down the hall to Trixie. She was always waiting with smoky eyes and a wagging tail.

Matters went even further. Trixie did not like being left alone with my divine wife. She got nervous. When she got nervous, she got aggressive. The problem was compounded when, in 1984, we got a third dog, another German short-hair, named Ginger. Trixie did not like having another dog in the house.

One weekend when my wife and I were at our rented house in Santa Cruz, I decided to stay over for another night. My paragon wife flew back to L.A. alone. When she entered the house, Trixie ran frantically looking for me. She did not find me. She began to growl at Martha and Ginger out of pure frustration. Then she lunged at Ginger, and then at Martha. She bit Martha.

Alex, my otherworldly wife, and Elena, our patient house-keeper, did what no human should ever do. They got in the middle of a dogfight. Worse, they got into the middle of a dogfight started by a jealous bitch who thought she had been spurned.

In a few seconds, Trixie had bitten my wife's wrist so badly that she had nicked the bone. She had gnawed into Elena's knee and cartilage. Then she went into the guest bedroom and growled.

When I flew home the next morning, Martha was at the vet getting her ear stitched. Alex was on the fifth floor at Cedars-Sinai Hospital, getting intravenous antibiotics. Elena was in a cast. Trixie was in the guest bedroom wagging her tail.

At the bottom line, I am still a human being married to another human being and Trixie is a dog. I offered to Alex to have Trixie executed by a firing squad in the backyard. My vision was of Marlene Dietrich walking slinkily to the post and exhaling a final, defiant puff. Needless to say, I could never have done it. But Alex is a saint, so she forgave Trixie. Elena is also a saint, and Martha is from another planet, and Ginger has a big heart, so they forgave Trixie, too.

The routine resumed after a few months. My wife leaves the house for meetings with high party officials at Paramount or UA, and Trixie and I lie in bed together. Through the haze of unconsciousness, I can feel rustling and burrowing under the covers. Then there are a warm chest and a cold nose pressing against my body. There is Trixie, limpid pools, and a warm lick across my nose.

For a few minutes each morning, I do not think about how much richer Michael Eisner is than I am, why my scripts never get made, why ABC has mistreated me so badly about *Amerika,* or why my pals all live in castles in Brentwood Park while I get older in my honky chateau. I don't think about anything. I just feel Trixie's warmth and see myself in those brown eyes.

Dogs know nothing of mortality. Trixie sees me and knows that I will be there forever, and she will be forever in my arms. For a few minutes every morning, I know it, too.

APRIL 22, 1986

Lunch at the Universal Commissary with Lucinda DeMott. She's just about our funniest, smartest pal. She and I sat only one booth from the Imperial Booth of Lew and Sid. It was awesome.

"I don't even try to find a decent man," Lucinda said. "It's a waste of time. There aren't any nice men in Hollywood. Why bother to look? Where's the advantage? Why look for something there aren't any of?"

"You can't live the rest of your life without men," I said. "Or maybe you can."

"No, I don't plan to," she said. "I'm moving to Hawaii in a few months. Then I'll find my dream man. He'll be really, really strong, and he'll really look great, only he'll be retarded. Not totally, but just so much that he'll never run away."

"Great idea."

"It was in some movie with Piper Laurie and Mel Gibson." Lucinda nodded. "They had great sex, and he was a carpenter to boot. That would be my dream man. A retarded guy who was also a handyman."

"What makes you think you'll find him in Hawaii?"

"Well, their alphabet has only thirteen letters, so how smart can they be?" she asked.

"Good point."

"The next best would be to marry a really, really rich man, and live in a house that had totally separate wings and never, ever see each other, and absolutely never have sex."

"Another great idea."

"I like to prepare for life as it is," she said. "There's no point dreaming."

APRIL 23, 1986

Yes, there is. A telephone call from my teacher. "Why haven't you been to class lately? The kids are restless. They miss you. They wonder where you are. Especially little Tammie. She says she really misses you."

Speaking of dreams, I also got a call from Sonya, Traci's younger sister, who goes to the University of Arizona.

"My teacher told me he heard your name over Radio Moscow," she said. "Shortwave. The guy said you were a right-wing ideologue for thinking up some miniseries. What's a right-wing ideologue?"

"Well, I'm not really a right-wing ideologue. . . ."

"Is it anything like a right-hand-drive Jaguar? I went out with a guy who had one of them, and it was so cool."

"It's a lot like that," I said. "I'll call you tomorrow."

"I'm coming into town tomorrow," she said, "so you can take me to dinner."

APRIL 24, 1986

A few little notes about my neighborhood: There are stop signs on several intersections near our little house. Like every other stop sign, they read STOP in giant white letters on a red background. However, unlike the stop signs in Grosse Pointe or Chevy Chase, these also say, in a very personal handwriting, ME FROM DOING IT AGAIN . . . PLEASE. It adds a little neighborly touch.

Even late in the afternoon or early in the evening as I head out to dinner, I always see gardeners finishing their daily rounds. They have giant hoses with high-pressure nozzles. They aim the blast of water at a few miserable dead leaves and blow them over to the gutter in front of the next-door neighbor's house. To move one one-eighth-ounce leaf a few feet, they routinely use one thousand gallons of water. This water has to be brought from the Owens Valley, three hundred miles away. It must be pumped by huge generators up and down mountains. The amount of gasoline and oil used to move water in California each day is six times what is used to light the lights and cool the buildings of Los Angeles. Dozens of people died building the aqueducts from the Owens Valley.

The Owens Valley itself was once one of the most productive, fertile valleys in the world. Now it is high desert, low scrub, a bombed-out, uninhabitable zone.

When I think that the water brought from there is used to move leaves a few feet, so that another set of gardeners can then move them a few more feet, I start to lose my mind.

Still, enough of that. Sonya, who brought me the cookies last Christmas Day, is waiting for me at Pina Fini. It's a supertrendy place on Beverly next to the fabulous Hard Rock Cafe. It has interior neon lighting and huge blowups of models with hollow cheeks and lifeless eyes. It's swell. On weekend nights, it is jammed with Iranians and the girls who want to meet them. In fact, the cute kids who come here have a name for this place. They call it "Penis Venus." I know the phrase doesn't exactly make sense. The real news would be if anything in L.A. *did* make sense.

Sonya and I sat under a twelve-by-twelve-foot portrait of a model who looked as if she had done enough blow to send all the water in Los Angeles *back* to the Owens Valley.

"Have you ever heard of someone really, really famous named Betsy Hamm?" Sonya asked. "Superfamous."

"I guess I haven't."

"She's the one who blew up the White House back in the sixties. Don't you remember her?"

"I really don't. Tell me more about it."

"Well," Sonya said, sipping her gin and tonic, "this is what happened according to our history teacher at Arizona. See, the hippies all loved the Beach Boys. That was hippie music. So the hippies all wanted to have a giant concert and the Beach Boys would play from the roof of the White House. It would be totally rad. And it would end the war in Vietnam, although I can't remember how it would do that."

"This is all starting to come back to me."

"So, then Nixon wouldn't let the kids have the party on the roof because he was really mean and against hippies and all. See?"

"It's sounding really, really familiar."

"So Nixon wouldn't let the hippies have the party on the roof of the White House, so they blew up the White House. Don't you remember that?"

"I sort of remember," I said. "Go on."

"So the FBI and the CIA tracked down the bombers and they found out that Betsy Hamm was the one who did it. Someone told on her or something. So they arrested her, only she wouldn't talk. So they put her in a really fancy penthouse apartment in Washington, and brought in champagne and caviar all around the clock, only she still wouldn't talk. They kept her there for two years. Finally, her family was so famous and so powerful that they got her out. And then she wouldn't even talk to them because they were really rich, and in the sixties, people didn't want to have anything to do with money. At least young people didn't."

"That part I remember perfectly."

"Good. So then when she got out, a big book publisher offered her like a million dollars or maybe two million dollars for her memoirs. And she said she didn't even want to talk to them, because she was a sixties chick and she didn't want anything to do with money, even though it's the eighties now."

"You know," I said, "now that you're telling me all of this stuff, I remember it all. I think I met Betsy Hamm at a Weather Underground cell meeting while I was working at the White House."

"What's the Weather Underground?" Sonya asked. "It sounds really neat, like some kind of really cool club."

"It is really, really neat. I'll tell you about that sometime when you're older."

"Okay," Sonya agreed. She's almost unbelievably agreeable. She does occasionally punch her boyfriend and knock out a tooth, but with me she's peaches and cream. "Can you help my friend Louise get into the picture business?"

"I doubt it."

"She's incredibly beautiful. She's so beautiful that she dropped out of our high school, Holy Innocents, when she was fifteen to start acting in porno movies. If you go to any video place, they'll have lots of her movies. It's really, really great how she became a star so fast."

"That really is great."

"And she had a Mercedes convertible when she was sixteen, and she used to come by the school and show off her car, and all the kids were so jealous."

"Far out."

"What's that mean?"

"Nothing."

"So, anyway, no sooner did she get really famous than the guys who used her in the movies got busted because she was like underage when she started doing the porno movies. So that wasn't good at all. So for a long time she worked for her dad, who has an insurance agency in Burbank, like answering claim letters and things, but then she got bored, and now she wants to get back into the movies, and I told her that maybe you could help her."

"Yes, well you'd better tell her I left town."

"Okay. Listen, can you help me get a job as a TV anchorperson? I would really love to have that kind of job. It would be great."

"Why the hell not?"

"Thanks, Ben."

April 28, 1986

Back to class at Birmingham High School. It's a slow day. The classroom has no windows at eye level. It's not air-conditioned. Frankly, it's too hot in this room. The boys and girls have a listless, dazed look. They listen to Walkmans, play cards, whisper to one another while the teacher talks to them about current events.

"I saw a guy walking out near Balboa Park who had on a T-shirt that had a big swastika and then a sign that said HITLER TOUR—WARSAW, PARIS, ROME," said André, a boy whose parents emigrated here from Russia. "It really made me mad."

"That's very, very interesting," the teacher mused. "What do you kids think about that T-shirt?"

"I think if I see him again I'm going to run him over," said André.

"I think that it's disgusting," a girl said without looking up from *Vogue*.

Jerry, an unusually smart boy who plans to go to Princeton if he can learn where it is located, had another opinion. "I think that this is a free country, and anyone who feels like it should be allowed to say anything he wants."

"Well, this is interesting," the teacher said. "Now let's have a show of hands. How many of you think that it's really disgusting for someone to wear a Nazi T-shirt and how many of you think it's his First Amendment right?"

"What's First Amendment mean?" asked Lynn, a boy who always wears an Iron Maiden T-shirt.

"Freedom of speech," the teacher said sweetly.

"Freedom to kill," added Chris, a very smart boy who sits near me and reads *Soldier of Fortune* on occasion.

About three-fourths of the class thought that the T-shirt

wearer should be run over. About three kids thought he should be able to wear the T-shirt with impunity. The rest kept listening to their Walkmans.

"Good," the teacher said. "Now let's go on with our discussion of the Philippines."

After class I asked her if she did not think that perhaps, on this one occasion, she might take a moral stance and frankly say that she thought that Nazi slogans were disgusting, and there were no two ways about it.

"I really don't think so," she said. "I like for them to make up their own minds."

"About Nazism?"

"About anything. I don't believe in a teacher actually trying to teach anyone any values. The kids should learn that themselves."

"How?"

"I don't know. Trial and error."

The man with the T-shirt would certainly have approved.

Still, this is L.A. I walked out to the car, past the newly cut grass. It smelled wonderful. One rarely gets to smell it in the hillsides of Hollywood. In the East, in the suburbs, it is taken for granted. If I ever started to think about all of the things from my childhood that were taken for granted and are now gone forever, I would not have time to do anything else. Anyway, why should I? Where's the deal in that? What's the percentage in nostalgia unless there's a writer and a director attached? I've got to start getting tough.

MAY 1, 1986

A slow day sitting by the pool thinking about whether I should make myself into an indentured servant, take up law again, and live indoors so that I can have a steady paycheck. Trixie, Martha, and Ginger sat around me, helping me to think.

Suddenly they started to bark frantically. At our back gate, where usually there are demented people from a nearby halfway house walking by wrapped in blankets, there was my pal Mark. Mark is a man who was thirty-one when I moved here in 1976. By a true miracle, he is still thirty-one. Since I came here, he has gone from being an official at MGM to being a real estate promoter to being a director to being a writer, the last redoubt of the confused. I shouldn't really say "being." I never know what he is "being." He's "acting." That's a better description.

Anyway, since I have known him, he has gone from life as a husband to life as a single man. That's what he wanted to talk about today. He never calls to tell me he's coming. He just shows up.

"I hear you're no longer being represented by Schloimie Schlepkis," Mark said. "He used to be my agent."

"Was he any good?" I asked. "He didn't do much for me."

"Look, darling, no agent ever does anything for anyone else but himself. Don't even expect it. Agents are for guys who are already successful. If you're not already successful, they aren't going to lift a finger to help you, pal. That's how Hollywood works. You think that agents are out there trying to make some new kid from Idaho into a successful writer? No fucking way, daddy-o. They're looking to latch on to someone who's already successful and steal him away from William Morris. That's how it works."

"Thank you for explaining it to me," I said.

"That's how most agents work. But Schlepkis is worse even than most agents. Schlepkis is so bad, I can't even find a word to describe him." Mark sat silently in the sunshine for a few minutes. Then he snapped his fingers. "The Antichrist. That's how I'd describe him. That's the only phrase that goes far enough. The Antichrist."

"I like it. It has a certain ring to it. Let's see if we can sell it on name alone."

"Maybe," Mark said, brooding as he looked at the pool.

"Who are you dating these days?" I asked.

"*Dating?*" he exploded. "*Dating? I'm not dating anyone. I'd* rather date Trixie than date any woman in Los Angeles."

"Trixie's taken."

"Look, let me tell you about dating. I saw this gorgeous girl at Morton's a few weeks ago. Gorgeous. Tall, long blond hair. A fucking knockout. So I asked Victor, the captain, who the hell she was. He says her name is Agnes. She's from Scotland or somewhere, and she's really a hot number. So I gave Victor a hundred, and he got her phone number for me. So I call her up, and I take her out to dinner at Morton's. I give Victor another hundred to make sure I get the best table, the little deuce near the door, where everyone can see what a knockout I'm with. Can you cop to it?"

"I'm hip."

"Okay. So I start to ask her about herself. First thing out of her mouth, she tells me she's had some very heavy boyfriends. Also some TV actor, and a whole slew of guys who own banks and insurance companies. 'I like to date successful men,' she tells me.

"So right away, I'm cut off just about at dick level. I mean, how the hell am I supposed to even come close to competing with people like that?"

"You're a lot more fun to talk to than those men."

"I'm also a lot more fun to fuck, I suspect," Mark answered. "But that's not how women here make their decisions. So while I'm thinking about that, she says, 'Look, I've probably had just about every really successful man in L.A. I'm twenty-four, and now I'm sort of at a crossroads in my life. You know what I mean?'

"So I'm thinking what I can do, and she says, 'Maybe you can help me get a job. I really need a job.'

"Okay. So I ask her what kind of job she wants.

"She says, 'I'd like a job that pays a really lot of money, where I can be really close to horses, where I can enjoy fine wine, and where I can collect great art.'"

"Is that all?" I asked. "Maybe she should enlist in the Army."

"Yeah," Mark agreed. "So I racked my brains for a while, and I said maybe she should be a broker for commercial real estate.

"'I don't know,' she says. 'I never really learned to add or subtract or multiply or divide. So it can't be anything with numbers.'"

"Has she tried Goldman, Sachs?"

"So I asked her what she thought she would like to do. 'I don't know,' she said. 'Anything where I can use my feet a lot. I'm really good with my feet, like with acrobatics or gymnastics or climbing trees or tap dancing. I can really do nice work at that kind of stuff.'"

"I'm sorry," I said. "I really am sorry."

"You're sorry?" Mark asked. "That dinner cost me three hundred bucks. Three hundred bucks. Can you dig? Plus, I had sent her roses the day before to get her primed. So when dinner's almost over, she says she has to leave because she has to do her toe exercises before she goes to sleep. So I ask her if she wants to do her toe exercises on me, and she walks out of the fucking restaurant. Out of Morton's, with all of those people looking at me. Wow. What a world."

"Maybe you should try to find someone else. Someone nicer."

"Fuck 'nicer,'" Mark said. "You know any *nice* girls who know how to give decent head? Any? Even one?"

"Fifth Amendment."

"Yeah. You go out with a nice girl, she doesn't even know how to make your dick hard. She just sort of brushes it, like touches it, and then she giggles, and that's supposed to make you hard. Then, she gives a big sigh and says, 'Oh, all right. I'll *kiss* you.'

"And then she puts her lips on your dick, like she's making this big sacrifice for her country, and doesn't move or anything, and then she lies back down as if she's just run a mile with full field pack. Then when you're balling them, they buck all around and make noises and crowd you out of the fucking room with their screaming and *crexing*. You can't even get a decent fantasy going. Then they cry.

"A nice girl? Don't fucking talk to me about nice girls, okay?"

"Okay."

"You know what I'd like to find? You know what I'd really and truly like to find?"

"No. What?"

"A really, really nice hooker, a high-class call girl, who was maybe twenty-nine or thirty, and had an idea of how to please a man and take care of him, and knew what was real and what was not. You know lots of call girls. Maybe you know somebody."

"I do know lots of ex-call girls," I said. "I'm not sure at all how happy you'd be with one of them. I think they've seen a lot of bad things happen in their lives. I think they must be pretty angry women. Even the ones who seem nice when you're paying them may not be quite as nice when you're not paying them. What do you think?"

"I think that the only women I ever have any fun with are call girls. Look, you go to a call girl. You know she's always gonna be right on time. You know you're always gonna score. Always. You know she's not gonna jerk you around trying to make it sound like she's got an interesting life when she's really a bookkeeper for a carpet company. You know what I mean? She's not gonna sit at Morton's and order a whole bottle of champagne and then tell you how much richer all the other men she's had are. You know what to expect, and it's pretty good."

"But it's for money," I said. "There's no real affection involved. Doesn't that mean anything?"

"You tell me something, Pop," Mark said. "You tell me how much affection's involved when you pick up a girl at Le Dome and bring her home. How much affection is there when you buy a girl a great dinner and even if she does ball you, you can't wait to get her the hell out of the house, and you'd rather jerk off when you come to think of it? How much affection do you think there is in a garden variety fuck these days?"

"I don't know." I looked longingly at Trixie. The conversation was making me wish I were in bed in a cool, darkened room, with her looking at me and wagging her tail.

"Not too goddamn much," Mark said. He got up and paced back and forth. He reminded me of a crazed bull, getting ready to charge. Even the dogs were getting visibly edgy, walking around in circles, picking up his frustration.

"A date today is like a fight. You know how the Navy says that a landing on a carrier is a controlled crash?"

"I've read that."

"Yeah, well, a date today, or a pickup, or anything where a man is out with a woman and sex is involved, yeah, a date today is like a controlled homicide. Both sides are trying to hurt the other as much as possible and still fuck each other. The women usually want to get fucked even more than the men. I'm not kidding. But they also want to cut the man's balls off while they're fucking him."

"I believe you," I said. One rarely gets to witness an outburst of such genuine emotion in Los Angeles, and I was happy to have the chance. Well, maybe not *happy*, but it was a change. For sure, for sure. Much better than "Have a nice day." Plus, it would come in really handy if I should ever need a reason to shoot myself.

"I met this woman at a bar in The Marina," he said. "She's really a killer. Tall, thin, with a big nose. With these really weird black eyes. So we've both had a couple of vodka gimlets, and I take her out for a walk. We're walking around, and she sticks her hand in my pocket and says, 'I want to fuck you. I want to fuck you more than I ever wanted anything in my life.'"

"That's a nice thing to hear."

"So just as she says that, we're in front of an apartment house on a canal, and it's got an 'open house' sign in front of it. She takes me by the hand and leads me into this little garden apartment. There's nobody in it. Nobody. So we creep around, and she yanks me into this closet and says, 'Fuck me. Right now.'

"So I say, 'I can't fuck you in this closet. What if someone comes in?' And she says, 'You want me to go down on you?' And before I can say a word, she's down on her knees copping my joint. And then when I'm done, she says, 'Ohmigawd, you just got come on my jeans. And they're from Jax, and I don't even know if come will come out of a pair of Jax jeans. How could you do that?'

"Meanwhile, she's still on her hands and knees, and I'm there with my dick hanging out at some apartment house where some Iranian is probably about to walk in.

"So then she says, 'Okay, it's your turn. Now fuck me. Right here on the floor.' And I say, 'I can't fuck you. You just went down on me two minutes ago. If you wanted to fuck me, you shouldn't have gone down on me so fast.'

"So she looks at her watch and she says, 'Well, how long will it take you to fuck me? I'm supposed to be at the academy for a screening at eight. I don't have all night.'

"I think I started to cry. Anyway, she says, 'By the way, I hope you're married, because I'm married to one of the biggest manufacturers of accessories in California, and I don't like to get involved with anybody who has less to lose than I do.'

"I told her I wasn't married, and she says, 'Ohmigawd, then you're gay, right? And now look what I've done. Ohmigawd, I've probably just killed myself. That's why you can't get it up, right? Because you're gay? Have you been to a doctor lately?'"

"I think you should consider going into a monastery."

"Or another town. People are just too goddamned mean in this town. Too much. A call girl, on the other hand, is totally different. She's nice all the time. Every time you see her, it's like the beginning of a relationship. You have to pay her, and that's all you have to do. She's never gonna make you feel like you suddenly made the worst mistake of your life and your blood is going to start flowing the other way in your body if you don't leave in two seconds.

"Plus, it's very economical. You pay a hundred and fifty bucks, but what's that in 1986? That's *bupkis*. Nothing. A nice dinner and a few drinks is that much, and you spend a few hours at it besides. So you lose all that time you spend with her that you could've spent working. How much is your time worth? Mine goes for about three hundred an hour, I figure. So a date could cost me a grand, easily. Very easily. There's no woman in L.A. who's worth a grand."

"Alex and Trixie. Martha and Ginger, too."

"Yeah, well, I'm beginning to see your point. I can cop to the whole business with the dogs and the wife now. It makes a lot of sense.

"But a hooker, a good call girl, is even better. It's like you're always at the second date of a really nice 1964-type relationship every time you see her. Both of you are being polite and nice, and there's no emotional risk, and if she's Miss Right, she gives head that makes you lose your mind. Very emotionally economical. Very financially sound. And no fucking crazies that make you want to run and hide. After a date these days, you feel like you've just visited a mental hospital. After you see a call girl, you feel like Tarzan."

"It's a very persuasive argument."

"So the chick from The Marina calls me at my office the next day. 'When are we gonna go out again?' she asks. 'I want to fuck you.'

"Mark," I said. "Have you considered accepting Jesus Christ as your own personal savior?"

"Yes," he said. "I have."

May 4, 1986

No school this morning, but a telephone call from little Tammie. "Hi, Mr. Stein," she cooed. "How are you?"

"I'm fine." I'm trying to be businesslike with her. Any other approach is too hazardous to my health.

"Listen, you know how you told me you had just written a script about a congressman who has an affair with a teenage girl?"

"Yeah." Jesus, did I tell her that?

"Well, I have to do a project about writers for my class over at

Birmingham High School. Could I option your screenplay, maybe for a few dollars? I don't think anyone else in class will think of doing that. Maybe for a month for ten dollars?"

"I have a better idea. How about murdering me, then using my body as a cadaver in your biology class and dissecting it? I doubt if anyone has thought of that either."

As I knew would happen, the next call was from my pal Mark. "Listen," he said, "forget about all that stuff about girls. It's beyond talking about already. Anyway, what I wanted you to know is about Carla Sing, that girl who used to be a waitress at Paramount's commissary. You remember her?"

"Sure. Great-looking Chinese girl. Really polite. Long black hair but she never got it in the fried shrimp."

"Exactly. Well, her boyfriend, this lighting man, just went away for a long vacation without her, so she stayed home and wrote a script just to pass the time."

"All right, Mark. How much did she sell it for?"

"So she took the script to a friend at Disney. . . ."

"Cut it out, Mark. Just tell me. Was it more or less than two hundred and fifty thousand?"

"Bingo. Exactly two hundred and fifty thousand. Another two hundred if it gets made. And English isn't even her native language and she never finished high school. . . ."

But I didn't hear the rest because I hung up.

Another call. The teacher. "The kids love you so much that they'd really like for you to be a chaperon at the senior prom weekend after next. Would you like to come?"

Would I like to come? At my own high school senior prom in Silver Spring, Maryland, the girl who was supposed to be my date couldn't go with me at the last minute. Her parents wouldn't let her go because I was Jewish. A kindly friend took pity on me and made his sister go to the prom with me. By the way, the kindly friend and the girl who couldn't go with me are now married, so go figure.

"Carol," I said, "I would dearly love to go to the prom with your kiddies. It would be a pleasure and an honor."

"Now don't forget. It's not this weekend, but next weekend."

"I won't forget."

Oh boy! With my gorgeous tall blond wife, my Porsche, my connections in Hollywood, this is going to be the best prom ever! Better yet, forty-one is the ideal age to attend the best prom ever.

Alex had to work late, so I went over to Le Dome to have a drink and flirt with the girls. Perfect. Absolutely perfect. There I sit, a full-on braino, looking like a full-on braino, no matter how hard I try to look like anyone else, and all around me are women so hard they use their hips to polish diamonds. I started to talk to one Asian woman. She told me she was the daughter of a German Nazi pilot and a Japanese woman. "I was born during the war," she said.

"You hardly look old enough to have been born during the war," I said.

"I'm twenty-two," she said.

"Well, that means you were born in 1964, and the war ended in 1945."

She gave me that withering look we brainos deserve for that kind of crack. "No," she said. "The war in the Pacific went on much longer. It didn't end until a few years ago."

Before I could even admit my obvious error, she turned away to talk to a black man dressed in black leather on her other side.

I turned to a woman on the other side. A truly beautiful woman with pale skin, deep blue eyes, and a wonderful figure. "May I talk to you?" I asked.

"Sure," she said.

She was Australian. She had been in America for a few months seeking her fortune. She had already been offered a Playmate spot. She had already been offered a million dollars to have the baby of a wealthy real estate developer.

I told her I was a writer. "A waiter?" she asked pleasantly.

"No, a writer."

"Oh." She paused for a long time, and then she added,

"Writers are all right. At least I don't think they carry disease the way a lot of other people do."

Very appetizing, and so I went back to Trixie.

On the way home, I had the feeling I often have: the world is a screaming insane asylum. Everyone I meet here is a nutcase of one kind or another. But really and truly scary. Not just a little bit dumb like in high school. Off-the-map nutso.

I'm so happy to be able to go back to my little house, with my big wife and the dogs. It's my refuge, shelter from the storm. What on earth do people do who don't have a home? They must be like dogs on the freeway divider, just running around crazily, scared out of their minds until they die.

MAY 6, 1986

A telephone call from the man in the pajama top about the civil rights project. I had begun to forget it even existed. "We have a potential writer in mind," he said. "Nosey Flynn. A really good-quality TV writer. He's done a lot of work for our TV division. A really outstanding guy. Like you. Very intellectual."

My partner Schmooey and I went over to the studio to see Maestro Flynn. Maestro Flynn was a fat, sweating man wearing a full Cleveland, a polyester suit of light blue, a white plastic belt, and white plastic shoes. He also had a beard with what looked like sesame seeds and part of a Big Mac wrapper attached.

"Before you tell me your idea," he said, "perhaps we could each take a few minutes to tune our instruments."

I started to tell him that it was not an "idea" but an actual true-to-life story that had really happened.

Alas, it was too late. He already was waving his arms in the air, inhaling deeply, and pressing his palms against his abdomen. After about thirty seconds, he stopped.

I told him about the three civil rights workers, Goodman, Chaney, and Schwerner, and how they had been murdered by a secret cell of the Ku Klux Klan. Nosey took more deep breaths, then got up and paced around the room.

"The way I see it, the heavies would be the civil rights workers themselves."

"I love it," Schmooey said.

"What the hell are you talking about?" I asked.

"Well, the way I see it is that the civil rights workers were just showing off, looking for a cause, without realizing how much they were upsetting the local people. They really deserved to die, and maybe the people who went to jail for killing them were the real martyrs."

"I hope you're kidding."

"I'm not kidding," he said, looking at me as if I were a third-grader in the remedial reading class at a school in Watts. "The obvious way to go would be to take the side of the civil rights workers. But in drama, you have to go with the surprise route, turn the tables on the viewer's expectations."

"Look. The whole point of the story is that the civil rights workers were standing up to incredible, outrageous victimization of black people in Mississippi in 1964. Black people were routinely lynched for looking crosswise at white women. They just disappeared if a white man wanted their land. They never got to vote. They basically had no rights. Goodman, Chaney, and Schwerner gave their lives to change all of that. That's the story. It's about how brave three young people were, not about how brave their killers were."

Nosey Flynn gave a weighty sigh.

"Look, Bill," he said, looking at me.

"My name's Ben."

"Right. Well, Ben, when I was an undergraduate at Yale, I ghostwrote the last three of the novels and books of poetry of Robert Penn Warren. That was where I learned about reversing

147

the obvious. Then, when I was at Yale Law School, I realized that the law is rarely a straight line."

"You were at Yale Law School?" I asked. "When?"

"Class of 1970," he said. "I was valedictorian of the class."

"I was in the class of 1970," I said. "I don't remember seeing you around."

"Well, it was a big class," Nosey said without missing a beat.

"There were only eighty people in our class."

"Well, I dropped out."

"How did you get to be valedictorian if you dropped out?"

Nosey heaved another sigh. "Look, is this '20 Questions' or what? Let's not think about details. You want me to do this or what?"

"I'd like to think about your approach, if I may."

Out in the parking lot, Schmooey started to scream at me in Hebrew. Then he translated. "This guy is studio-acceptable. Who the fuck cares where he went to school?"

"I don't care where he went to school. I care that he's lying his head off at our first meeting, before he's even done any work. That's what I care about."

"How do you know he's lying? Maybe you're wrong." He paused for a moment, and I know he was about to say, "Maybe *you're* lying."

"I'll talk to you later, Schmooey," I said, and I went home.

What a world. Because I wasn't lying, I'm now suspected of lying. Because I caught out a boastful nut, and because that schmuck is "studio-acceptable," I'm the one under suspicion. In *Lost in America*, Isaac Singer says, "Hollywood is an insane asylum. A real one." He was smart to stay on the Upper West Side eating his herring at cafeterias.

When I got home, I telephoned Gloria McHugh, the head of alumni affairs at Yale Law School. She verified for me that indeed no Nosey Flynn had ever even applied to Yale Law School, much less been a student.

I called Schmooey and told him. "It doesn't matter," he said. "He already called to say he wouldn't work with someone who questioned his honor."

"Good riddance."

"No. Now who are we gonna get to write the thing? When are you gonna learn that the only line that counts is the bottom line? You've been here ten years, and you still don't understand Hollywood at all. It doesn't matter if he's a liar and he's crazy. We get paid our producer's fee anyway, just as soon as he starts writing. That's the part that counts.

"The bottom line, *boychick*. This isn't a game. It's a business. I'm beginning to wonder if you're ever gonna understand that."

MAY 7, 1986

Lunch on a scorching day at the Universal Commissary. There are no windows and the air-conditioning is working perfectly. Up on the long wall facing the door are the usual huge translucent photos of Universal's stars. It's a sign of my life that when I came here in 1976, I could name virtually every face on the wall. Now they are Brat Packers, stars of TV shows I have never seen, women in Salvation Army chic who look as if they share needles, people I do not want to know.

Nevertheless, Lucinda DeMott is in a good mood, as usual.

"I got a check last Friday for three MOWs I worked on when I was at *Talkstar*. They weren't going to pay me, but they finally did. A hundred and ten thousand. All in one check. It was fabulous. I held that check and looked at it, and I felt like a Republican. Now I see why people like being rich.

"So then I took it to the Bank of America here at Universal City, to put in my account. And the tellers were all looking at it and going ooh and ahh, and then they had to get some kind of approval from some little jerk who's the assistant manager or something, so they got that approval, and he looks at the check, and he says, 'Well, Tom Selleck has a bigger check than this every week when he's in production, and Sid Sheinberg has bigger checks than this every week whether the studio's making money or not.' So for a minute I felt as if my check wasn't that big at all, but then I thought that my check was probably five times what that assistant manager makes in a year, so fuck him anyway."

"You got that right," I agreed.

"Anyway, I've figured out a way to get really and truly rich," Lucinda said with great conviction, waving a cigarette around as if she were about to start conducting the Dresden Symphony in Mozart's Symphony No. 41. "It's called 'Lifescript.' See, everybody's interested in learning how to write a script, and also everybody's interested in learning how to improve their lives.

"So we get a program which has huge classes all around the country, and a book, and we have people write out a script which simply says how their lives have gone so far, and then how they would like them to go for the rest of their lives. People have to dramatize the steps by which they're going to get what they want out of life. That way, if it's totally out of the blue, like expecting to win the lottery, people can be told that their 'Lifescript' is unconvincing and they have to revise it until they can show the instructor and themselves that what they have in mind can possibly be done and that it's realistic considering what's happened earlier in the script. That is, they can't get away with showing something in the script that shows them as completely different people from the kinds of people they used to be. Using who they really are, they have to pull their lives together to be the kind of people they want to be. Isn't that great?"

"Lucinda, it's incredible," I said, and I meant it.

"Oh, great," Lucinda said, clasping her hands together. "Now I know we can't fail."

We ate in a kind of excited silence for a moment and then we saw Larry Kasdan shuffle in. Larry is a talented fellow who has been able to make a fortune in Hollywood writing and directing, among other things, *The Empire Strikes Back, The Big Chill,* and *Silverado.* Larry is a bright guy, a cheerful guy, the kind of guy who shines with success and confidence. I don't know that he'll be a taker for "Lifescript." He's already doing well enough writing scripts for a million dollars for a draft, a set, and a polish. He does not need to pay us four hundred dollars to learn how to write a script.

Lucinda looked at him and smiled widely. "That gives me another idea," she said. "I think that to smooth out the differences in the society, we should have a maximum wage. Not a minimum wage, but a maximum wage. That way, we can be sure that no one is getting a truly outrageous amount of money for doing something that anybody could do."

"Another winner," I said.

"I'd set it at a million dollars a year," Lucinda said. "Even with a pool man twice a week, and two Mercedes and a house in the Colony, a family should be able to get by on a million dollars a year."

"I couldn't agree more," I said.

"Some people think that you need to have people like Sid earning five million a year to keep Universal going," Lucinda said. "I think they'd do it for a million a year. After all, they probably love their work, too. It's not just the money."

"I agree. For a million dollars a year, if necessary, we can import Korean workers to do the jobs. A million a year should at least bring in Mexican and Salvadoran immigrants who want to run studios."

"We have a big scare here at Universal," Lucinda said abruptly in a hushed voice. "Someone apparently sent a note to Lew and Sid threatening to kill 'eighty of your top executives' if he didn't get a screenplay gig immediately."

"'*Eighty* of the top executives'? How many does Universal have?"

"Well, at first we thought it was a joke," Lucinda agreed. "But then we thought, well, there are all of those buildings at the back of the lot, and nobody has any idea of who's in them. What if they're stuffed with executives from the forties and fifties, still making secret decisions?

"There was a sign up on lampposts all over Universal City this morning. I saw them on my way to work. They say PLEASE. OUR DAD IS MISSING. HELP US FIND HIM. Then there's a photo of a guy who could be anybody on the Universal lot. My theory is that the guy simply vanished on the Universal lot. Last week we got a handout from the studio security department. There was a flyer with a photo of a man and the flyer said he had raped someone in the Black Tower, and that if anyone saw him they shouldn't try to apprehend him, but they should call studio security and they would come arrest him.

"The joke is that the guy looked like every gaffer and every lighting man on every set at Universal. He also looked a lot like the missing dad."

We ate more of our food, and then Lucinda had another thought. "My nephew wants to come from Charleston and live in Los Angeles," she said. "He wants to be a geologist. I told him he was crazy to want to come here and do anything but work in the picture business. You agree?"

"I agree entirely. If you're here and you're not in the picture business, you might as well not be here." I thought about that for a minute and then had to add the truth. "There's no point in living here if you're not in the picture business," I repeated. "There's also no point in being here if you are in the picture business."

On the way out, I felt a little furry paw reach out and touch mine. It was attached to a little tight body and a little clever face. You guessed it.

"Are you producing anything here on the lot?" Marcie asked.

"No. Just having lunch."

"If you hear of anyone looking for a fifteen-year-old ingenue, tell him about me," she said. "If I get the part, I'll owe you one."

"One what?"

"Something nice," she said. "Because I feel that now you really truly know me."

"Yes, I believe I do."

MAY 9, 1986

Before I came to Hollywood, I used to laugh at superstition. To me, the Jivaro Indians in their patch of jungle were hilarious with their rituals and their taboos. I, a modern man, lived by logic and experience.

However, now that I am a Jivaro Indian, in that little patch of jungle bounded by the Golden State Freeway, the Ventura Freeway, the Harbor Freeway, and the Pacific Ocean, I believe in the occult and the unpredictable with all my heart.

How else to explain a small miracle. On my way to the Universal parking lot I ran into my pal Al. He wanted to know if I would be free to play a part in his sitcom, *Charles in Charge*, next week.

"Not that small a part either," Al said. "About thirty lines. A whole week's work at SAG minimum. Fifteen hundred right off the bat. More with residuals."

My favorite Hollywood superstition is that you must never put any pictures up on your walls. If you do, you will be sure to be fired right away. You must always act as if you were just there temporarily, just passing through. "Act like you're a Guatemalan who just might get a green card if you stay in town long enough," Michael Chinich once told me about Hollywood. "Be scared all the time, and never take anything for granted. That way, nothing bad will happen to you."

Isn't Hollywood great?

Well, anyway, I acted like I was real down at the mouth and sad, and look what happened! A small part in a sitcom! Can't do better than that, can you? Well, can you?

MAY 14, 1986

I love acting. Maybe that's the secret reason why I stay here. Maybe some magical hidden force is keeping me here to become an actor. Not a famous actor, mind you, but just an actor. "God, I'm an actor. An actor acts!"

I'm beginning to suspect that's Hollywood's secret. Lee Rich gets the best table at Morton's, and Mark Goodson has the cutest girls at Morton's, and Kirk Kerkorian and Lew Wasserman are the richest people at Morton's, but the actors, eating their fruit salad out of polystyrene containers, are the ones having a really fine time. The ones who are actually or potentially on stage are the lovers, and everyone else is just a well-paid, or poorly paid, voyeur.

Anyway, I did my acting gig for *Charles in Charge*. I played a cruel banker who turns down the leading character, a twenty-year-old college student, when he applies for a student loan. We rehearsed for four days in a huge stage at the very back of the Universal lot, almost to Burbank. I got to know the stage manager and the director and the cameramen and camerawomen, and the wardrobe people, the other actors, the stand-ins, the makeup men and women, even the unit publicist. They were having an incredibly good time, laughing and scratching, doing what they were put on earth to do—and who in the whole rest of the world can make that boast?

We would read our lines at a table, pounding it for emphasis, and then we would have a run-through, and then we would try to memorize our lines. Because I am a newcomer, and because I am seated at a desk, I was allowed to keep my script lines in front of me as if they were loan documents. That made it easier. Still, this time, unlike my stint in *Ferris Bueller*, I was required to actually *act*.

That is, I had to change my facial expression, say some lines with greater or less emphasis, try to become at least slightly different from what I really felt like being. The director would walk over to me and say, "Can you tweak the word *Charles* a little bit?" or, "Now when you come to 'Fat chance,' really spike it right down her throat."

I tried, and I liked it. It's not bad taking direction if you feel the director is on your side.

Today was taping day. Normally, a sitcom would be finished with taping by now and would be on what is called "hiatus" until it would start taping for the fall again in July or August. But *Charles in Charge* is a syndicated sitcom. It will play first on TV stations unaffiliated with the network, or at least not at prime time in an ad hoc *Charles in Charge* network that will have little or no connection with one of the three real networks. Fine with me. Frankly, I enjoyed it so much that it would be fine with me if it only played in Anchorage.

Anyway, today was taping day. First we did a run-through without an audience. Then an audience of recruits caught walking down Hollywood Boulevard and impressed into service at Universal was brought over for the afternoon taping, which is called "dress," as if it were "dress rehearsal" but it isn't, and then there was an "air" taping, for which several busloads of high school students had been brought in.

Frankly, it was swell. Outside, this whole week, the sky has been leaden and overcast with an unseasonal May storm. It was even chilly in the middle of the afternoon, which is unheard of for L.A. in May.

But in Stage 6, the temperature was always perfect. There was always a friendly face ready to talk about anything one felt like talking about, as long as it had to do with Hollywood. There was always a table with fruit and cookies and candy bars and sodas and doughnuts. There were always bright lights and someone to tell you how good you were.

There was even a dressing room off the main stage with my name on it, and a little couch and a desk and a telephone. Next to my dressing room was the dressing room of a lovable Irish actor, a hilarious trouper who did impressions for the whole cast and crew when things got slow.

When we actually started to do our roles in front of an audience, I took a huge swig of paregoric, and then adjusted my little brain for action. Frankly, I was too excited to be nervous. Anyway, this is tape, so if I make a mistake, they can always do it again.

Scott Baio, the man who was applying for the loan, and his employer, a lovely woman named Sandra Kearns, sauntered into my ersatz office. I mocked and belittled them, then sent them home without their loan. I acted as if I had done it a thousand times before, and Scott and Sandra acted as if I belonged there as much as if I were Edward Arnold. The audience laughed, and no one got up and screamed, "He's an impostor. Send him back to the Federal Trade Commission. Make him be a lawyer in Washington again!" In fact, the audience roared.

In the second act, I was even meaner and crueler, and the audience liked it even better, laughing and whistling.

After the audience left, we did "pickups," changing this or that detail, fixing flubbed lines, mixing memory with desire, breeding lilacs in the dead land, you know the whole drill.

Then I changed back into my "street clothes," and I was expelled from Eden. It was sad. I cried on my way home, although to be honest, I cry all the time anyway.

Inside that stage, I had a family, even if it was only for five days. The family took care of me, supported me, laughed at my lines, surrounded me with their interest, and I did the same back to them. When I think of the solitary, pitifully atomized life of the writer-producer-pitchman and compare it with what I was able to do this past week, when I contemplate the rush of excitement at being before a crowd on a lit stage in a sound stage and compare it with the empty feeling of pitching to a twenty-three-year-old production executive who is sticking paper clips in his ears when you talk to him, I feel frightened at the choices I have made. Still, it may not be too late.

On taping day, after wardrobe had fixed my banker's suit, after makeup had put "mean number 3" on my forehead, while lighting was struggling with the arc lamps to make me look just ruthless enough, while the cameramen and director were looking through lenses at me, the stage manager asked, "Are you comfortable, Ben?"

Oh, yes. Very comfortable. In the center of the universe that is Stage 6, how could I have been more comfortable?

I may have to talk to Granddad about this. This could be the time to make use of Granddad's providence and generosity to change careers. I'll have to call the Morgan Guaranty Trust Company in the morning.

Meanwhile, I have to start thinking about what to wear to the Birmingham High School Prom. I only have one tux, the one I bought in 1963 when I was pledging Alpha Delta Phi fraternity at Columbia, but maybe I should buy a cummerbund with a guy on a surfboard and SURF NAKED on it. I want this to be perfect.

MAY 15, 1986

How Hollywood works. This morning I awakened with a killer idea. Killer. It would be a love story set at the Democratic National Convention in Chicago in August of 1968. A high school from downstate Illinois would have a field trip to visit Chicago. While they were staying in Chicago, near the convention site, riots would break out. An air of unreality would descend over everything. A sullen, James Dean–like high school boy and his delicate, withdrawn female high school teacher would get caught in the riot and have to fight their way back to their hotel. In the meantime, the rest of the group would go back to downstate Illinois. In the brief, disconnected idyll that followed, the pair—the teacher and her student—have a torrid affair. Then they go back to Moline, or wherever they came from, and they resume their normal lives, immensely richer for the experience on that American *Walpurgis-nacht*.

I was so stirred by my story line (well, *somebody* has to like my ideas) that I called Michael Z., a high official at Paramount, and prevailed on him to meet me, even though most people will not take spur-of-the-moment meetings today, and induced him to see me.

We rendezvoused at his office and I started to tell him the story. "Wait a minute," he said. "You want a costume drama? A period piece?"

"Well, sort of a period piece," I said.

"You mean the women would be wearing hippie gingham dresses and things?"

"No, I mean clothes like today's only a little different."

"Nobody'll do a period piece today," he said. "Nobody."

"What about *Hair*?"

"Didn't make money."

"What about *Animal House*?"

"It was a comedy."

"What about *The Godfather*?"

"Adventure piece."

"Well, this is an adventure piece with love thrown in."

"Won't work."

"What about *Love Story*?"

"That was twenty years ago or something."

"Still, it was a period piece and it made money."

"Well, nobody cares about hippies anymore anyway."

"Our heroes won't be hippies. In fact, they're quite antihippie, as a matter of fact."

"Can't do it. We're looking for things that are fresh and new."

"This is new. It's just set in another time, like in *Star Wars*."

"Sorry. Come back when you think of something new."

This is Hollywood. When you try to sell something, a development executive will come up with every reason in the world why it can't work. There's no reason too silly to be used as a door to be slammed in your face. It does not matter if the development executives have no notion at all of what they are saying. It does not compute if their reasons have no connection with reality or even if they do not know the box office history of movies. Above all, do not expect any response based on artistic merit. Neither logic nor art has any weight. All that matters is that the development guy wants to say "no" and thinks up reasons to say no, and the reasons can change from minute to minute, have no internal or external consistency, cannot be understood or predicted, and are totally random.

To earn his living, the Hollywood writer/pitchman must navigate unknown and changing shoals, passing through an *in terrorem* standard of how his stories must be crafted, essentially gambling, with the odds always against him, and always being changed to be even more against him.

For example, I know that if I were to return to Michael in a week with a story not set in a period and not involving costumes, however slight, he would turn it down for a whole new set of reasons. If I then referred to the Chicago riots story, he would forget what he had said.

Most punishing of all, if I came in with that Chicago riots love story in one hand and Jane Fonda in the other and Stanley Kubrick between my teeth, there would be no jive talk about period pieces and what can't be done.

In other words, it's a completely unpredictable, unstable way to earn a living.

I considered all of that as I walked out of Michael's office and into the sunshine beating down on me. *I'll never pitch again*, I thought. *Never, never, never. I'll call the Morgan bank and start drawing on Granddad's trust, embarrassing as that might be.*

In the parking lot, I ran into yet another Michael. This one works in television, and I used to work with him on *Mary Hartman* years ago. (Almost all men in Hollywood are named Michael.)

"How ya doin'?" he asked. He was opening the door to a red Ferrari Mondial.

"I'm fine," I answered. "What are you doing?"

"Oh, maybe you didn't know. I own the syndication rights to *The Skeleton and the Boogie Man*, and now I have three more action shows on the network. I divide my time between our house in Aspen and our house on Martha's Vineyard. If you ever have any ideas, gimme a call."

Now, if he really has syndication rights to a major show like *Skeleton* and three network hour shows going on at the same time, he's down for about a hundred thousand a week. Maybe more. That's worth putting up with a lot of terror to get.

If I got into that charmed circle, my American Express bills would be like feathers. I could live on Martha's Vineyard, too, and spend all my time walking the salt marshes with Trixie. If I could just pass through that maze of terror at the pitch meeting, I would never have to do it again. I would be free of all of them, but only by somehow understanding what they want and selling it to them.

My very smart friend Eric Alter told me a story about a psychiatrist who did a study with two sets of rats. Set A was fed regular small amounts whenever each rat in the set jumped a small gap in the cage. Set B was fed much larger amounts, but only at random intervals, and only at unpredictable times when each rat jumped the gap.

Then the psychiatrist stopped feeding both groups when they jumped the gap. Set A refused to jump any longer. Set B, who had been randomly but richly fed, continued to jump until they died.

MAY 17, 1986

Ashes, ashes, all fall down.

The law of compensation, or the sadism of some cruel little imp, or something, has been hard at its fucking work.

Yesterday, Friday afternoon, I got a mournful call from my partner on the civil rights workers project. "Schecky [whom you know as the man in the black pajamas] has decided not to make the project after all," Schmooey said. "That's it. *Gurnicht.*"

"How can that possibly be?" I screamed. "They said we had a deal. They've been jerking us around about it for almost a year."

"I know," he said with the truly lugubrious tones which no one but an Israeli can even touch. "But he says now it's too serious, too sad. Besides, he heard you were a prima donna to work with."

"Who'd he hear that from?" I asked.

"Nosey Flynn, of course," said Schmooey.

"That fat jerk-off."

"Yeah, well, listen, it wasn't meant to be, so it wasn't meant to be. We try other places, we try to make it happen in other studios, eventually it will."

"I think we should sue them. They took it, made us change position in reliance, used up our assets of time and goodwill."

"Benjy, forget about it. It's a small town. We go on. We sell it somewhere else. Eventually someday we do another project with Schecky and maybe even with Nosey Flynn. You never know what's gonna happen. It's a small town."

Dinner at Morton's. Alex and I sat by the window and watched the usual Friday night "Encino night" crowd come in. There were a few agents from ICM, one table with what I think was George Hamilton, one table of Peter Morton's rich English pals. Other-wise, there were legions of wealthy rack jobbers, masters of the children's ready-to-wear business, swimsuit makers by the hundred, and their girlfriends and wives, all peering and furious-looking, all going to the ladies' room every five minutes, all looking as if they had come up from the showroom for a few minutes of air and then would be right back to bargain and shriek.

From our little perch next to the window, we could see the Rolls-Royces pull up in monotonous, showy procession. The men got out wearing leather trousers. The women also got out wearing leather trousers. They looked tough and scary and boring at the same time.

The few agents loitering at the bar had an entirely different attitude. They were all thin, all on edge, all seeming to walk only on the balls of their feet, all bantam cocks ready to come out fighting or perhaps dancing at any second, dervishes of ambition and energy, an ambition so palpable that it is even built into their posture. Jimmy Cagney doing deals for hot screenwriters is what their attitude said.

An agent came by and patted me on the back. "So I hear you have a piece of *Amerika,*" he said. "Nice going."

"I hope they make it," I answered.

"A little late for that." He smiled. "They started making it two weeks ago."

Fantastic! At long last, something I was connected to, no matter how slightly, will get made.

That perked up the meal. We talked about opportunities that getting a miniseries made might offer.

"Probably what it'll offer is that all the people in the 'peace' organizations will never like you again, and you'll be even more of an outsider than you are now," Alex said.

"Thanks."

"It doesn't matter. If they think they'll be able to make money from you, they'll still talk to you. They'll still buy things from you. And you'll still get deals."

When we got home, there were three messages on our

answering machine. All of them were from my teacher. "You'd better have a pretty good excuse for why you missed the prom," she said in the final one. The first two said, "Where are you? Why aren't you here at the prom?"

I felt my stomach fall to the floor. I felt my balls go into my abdomen. In a frenzy, I called her. "What are you talking about?" I demanded. "Proms are on Saturday nights. All of my proms when I was a child were on Saturday nights."

"Not anymore," she said. "Not here in California. Our proms are on Friday nights. Have been for twenty years. It was a great prom, though. I'll show you the pictures."

Goddammit to hell. That prom was the only chance I ever had for a perfect high school dance, and now it's gone.

MAY 19, 1986

The Resurrection and the Life.

A telephone call at 9:00 A.M. A cheery woman's voice said, "Hi. Is this the Ben Stein who was in *Ferris Bueller's Day Off?*"

To make a long story short, a wonderful commercial director saw me in the rough cut of *Ferris*, which I have not even seen yet. He thought I was the most perfect nerd he had ever seen. Now he wants to make me a player in a commercial for Godfather's Pizza. I'll be dressed up like an out-of-control loser in chartreuse silk pajamas, lying on a leopard skin couch, eating pizza. I like it. I like it a lot.

While I did pirouettes around the room with Trixie, the phone rang again. Robbie Wald, a producer whom I had met before at The Palm, had an idea. "I want to do a movie about a love affair between a boy from Malibu and a rich girl from Yale. The affair never quite works, and neither of them ever quite get over it. It's about obsession, longing, and loss. Are you interested?"

Is the Pope Polish?

I felt so good I called up Stacey and Traci to invite them to lunch at the Hard Rock Cafe. I love to see their little puppy faces when I'm happy. Just as I was leaving, the telephone rang again.

"Hi, giggle, giggle," said a girl's voice. "This is Wendy Klipspringer from Birmingham High School. We just wanted to remind you about the ceremony tonight, giggle, giggle."

"What ceremony might that be?"

"Oooh, giggle, giggle, I was afraid of that. We're planning to give you a big award, giggle, giggle, for being a friend of the school and everything, giggle, giggle. Maybe a consolation prize for missing the prom, too, giggle, giggle."

"This is the first I've heard about it."

"Well, can you come anyway?"

"Yes, yes I can, and I will."

So, so, so. I love this. I can go back after all.

All of these little fragments all at once. The wildly scattered dreams that are my reality are touching each other, making a wonderful smooth ball of anything-can-happen.

Who would ever dream that acting gigs, a screenplay, even going back to high school could ever happen in one day? Lemme tell you something, buster: it would never happen if I were working at a law firm or at the Federal Trade Commission. Once you get sealed up in that box of adult, day-to-day office living and working, there's no scope to dream, no room for maneuver to make your dreams come true.

When I got out of school, I went to work in an office in Washington, D.C. Immediately, a terrible truth dawned upon me. In school, I had been able to spend a large part of each day roaming about outside, in Sligo Creek Park, on Elm Street, on the New Haven Green. As an adult, I would live in shadow except for an hour at lunch. I would be a galley slave, even if I earned a living wage. The outside, the freedom of each day, would be a dim memory of youth. It was a killing thought.

Then I discovered Hollywood. Here, I found, it was possible to earn a living, be involved in the affairs of the town, not be a hermit, see great distances, and not stay locked in an office.

Or, to put it another way, here you can earn the paycheck of an adult and live the life of a child.

Here, I can work for a few hours per day, and still have time to hang out with Stacey and Traci, eat Chinese food with Sara, make jokes with Rich Procter, swim while Trixie lies on the pool deck in the sun. This is a dream life. Like any dream life, it also has its nightmares, like broken deals, story standards that simply cannot be met, a wildly unpredictable, random way of earning a living. But I could not expect it to be otherwise: I asked for a life beyond the bounds of the probable.

If I am not really successful here—and I assure you, I am not—it's my own fault. It *is* a business. I may treat it like a dream state, but it is a business, and the people who see it as such make the big dollar. The lucky part is that even with seeing it as a dream state, I can still make enough to pay the pool man and buy lunch for Stacey and Traci. Plus, some sweet day, by luck and magic, just by dreaming the magic words, the duck may come down from the sky with a hundred dollars.

The picture business may be a business and not a dream, but it still needs dreamers to put fuel into its belly. I am ready, should the call ever come.

Yes, yes, yes. This insane place, where nothing makes sense, is where I belong. My life makes no sense either, so where else should I be? I'm out here doing all of the things my parents told me led to ruin, and I'm still current on the mortgage and the American Express bill. I'm living in plastic land, and my life has the plasticity I always wanted, the good kind, as in the ability to be molded into whatever I so desire. That means spending a Tuesday afternoon racing down a street lined with royal palms to meet two college girls at the Hard Rock Cafe and laugh.

There is no Granddad. I never even knew either of my

grandfathers. Alex's grandfathers were soybean farmers in Oklahoma and Arkansas. There's only a confused haze of reality and fantasy, and walking in the sun and thinking long thoughts.

Anyway, that's on a good day.

ABOUT THE AUTHOR

Benjamin J. Stein is a native of Washington, D.C. He graduated from Columbia College and Yale Law School. He worked as a trial attorney, university teacher, White House speechwriter, and *Wall Street Journal* columnist. In 1976, he moved to Hollywood, where he has worked as a freelance writer and observer of many different fields, including high school, finance, and mass culture. He lives in the Hollywood Hills with his wife and son, adopted since this diary was completed.

He is the author of twelve books, including *DREEMZ, 'Ludes, The View from Sunset Boulevard,* and *Her Only Sin.*

Stein is a frequent contributor to *Barrons, Penthouse, Elle, GQ, The New York Times Magazine,* op-ed page and business section, and *The Washington Post.* He is active in the animal-rights movement.

He consults on complex corporate reorganizations, writes extensively about the law of securities and teaches about libel. He also writes and produces screenplays when he can.